TEN THOUSAND
HOURS IN PARADISE

VOLUME I: ARRIVAL

ANDREW M. CRUSOE

Mahalo nui Mimi & Dan!

Enjoy!

—Andrew

ISBN-13: 978-1-985-69435-4
ISBN: 1-985-69435-2

Version P1–20181107
Released by Aravinda Publishing

Cover features two photos of Hawaii by the author, as well as elements
from a photo by MODIS LRRT at NASA GSFC: http://bit.ly/hi2003
Book interior features a photo taken by NASA's Landsat 7. Mahalo to
the Hawai'i Institute of Geophysics & Planetology for providing this
royalty-free image via their site: http://hawaiiview.higp.hawaii.edu

Cover design, typesetting, and map revisions by the author.

DEDICATION

To the native Hawaiians who brought the healing principle of
ALOHA to this planet, changing the world forever.

THE ISLAND OF HAWAI'I

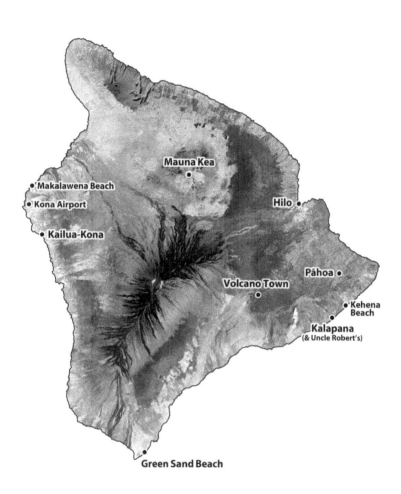

Mauna Kea

Makalawena Beach

Kona Airport

Hilo

Kailua-Kona

Pāhoa

Volcano Town

Kehena
Beach

Kalapana
(& Uncle Robert's)

Green Sand Beach

20 km
20 mi

MAHALO

I radiate deep gratitude to everyone who helped make this book possible. If it isn't completely clear yet, everything in this book actually happened. However, that isn't to say that my memory is perfect, and some events may differ from others' recollections. In pursuit of accuracy, I have recalled everything to the best of my ability, cross-referencing from my journals, correspondence, and photographs. Only the names have been changed, because that's apparently what one does when one writes a memoir.

Yet this book is unlike any memoir you have ever read: it is a taste of TRUE ADVENTURE on the most remote population center on the planet, a place that I have been honored to call my home. Thank you, Hawai'i. I realize now that you are indeed alive, and I feel such gratitude for our connection. You have given me greater awareness of how I relate to the Earth, to the life on it, and to myself. Truly, you have inspired me forever, and I hope my story within this book will inspire the reader, too.

So take a deep breath, and hold onto your heart.

CONTENTS

CHAPTER 1

TOUCHDOWN IN KONA

As MUCH AS I'VE REFLECTED on the beginnings of my journey, I cannot pinpoint the exact moment that I started dreaming about the Hawaiian Islands. To me, it felt like a foregone conclusion that I would someday go, as if it were destiny.

The history, art, and music of the islands had called out to me since my teenage years, especially the music of Israel Kamakawiwoʻole, whose platinum-selling cover of *Somewhere Over The Rainbow* rocked the world music scene in 1993.

I was age seven when the song hit, but it didn't get much airplay in rural Wisconsin where I was living at the time. When I did finally hear the song in my late teens, it touched me deeply. I felt the power in Israel's words. Sometimes it would move me so deeply that tears would form in my eyes, even in public, and I would quickly blink them away before anyone would notice.

How could this man, who almost always sang in a language I didn't even know, move me to tears?

In many ways, Hawaii is the exact opposite of where I spent most of my formative years in Northern Wisconsin, where winters would sometimes dip down to -40°F and snowstorms were a serious driving hazard.

The seasonality of the Upper Midwest was often awe-inspiring and beautiful to me. The summers and autumns I spent enjoying the lakes and forests were treasures of my childhood. But as adolescence dawned on me, I realized that I was living with roughly six months of cold weather per year, and it was starting to wear me down. So when my father had an opportunity to move us back to Fremont, California, the city I was born in, I felt a mixture of trepidation and raw excitement.

We moved in early August, hauling most of our valuables two-thirds across North America to the West Coast. While there, I taught myself the basics of website development, reconnected with my numerous cousins, and even made some short films with them, cultivating a love of filmmaking that I still have to this day. And nearly four years later, we did it again in the opposite direction.

I'll save the details of that story for another time, but in retrospect, I often wonder if my propensity for going outside of my comfort zone was inspired by my family culture. After all, I had no less than seven different addresses across six different cities before I turned fifteen, and I strongly feel that moving so often forced me to become more adaptable and comfortable with change. In fact, it wasn't until writing this book that I realized how profoundly the experience of being an outsider again and again shaped me and prepared me for my solo travels as an adult, including my journey to Hawaii that would change me forever.

After a few years back in Wisconsin, the long winters once again wore on me, and I couldn't help but feel that it was time to live somewhere with milder seasons. So when I graduated from college, I shot out of the state like a spring from a broken pocket watch, bouncing around with about as much predictability, as I used websites like Craigslist and Couchsurfing.com to explore parts of North America that I'd never seen before. Nearly 10,000 kilometers and five and a half months later, I returned home with a new courage and sense of self that I hadn't had before.

That journey deserves a book of its own, but even as I stretched myself through those experiences, a bigger goal loomed in the back of my mind: Hawaii.

The first concrete record I have of my fascination with Hawaii is a journal entry from mid-2007 mentioning how I loved the Hawaiian language. And about a year later in that same journal,

I described "a strange connection with Hawaii," almost as if I had "been there before..."

The next mention of Hawaii didn't occur until three years later, when I wrote down a one-line affirmation:

It is my mission to reach financial freedom. I will travel to Hawaii and Europe.

As time went on, my goal to go to Hawaii made its way into my daily affirmations, and as I grew into myself, I realized that going to that remote archipelago wasn't just something I *wanted* to do; it was something that I had to do.

Through all of my travels, I'd learned how my intuition often possessed an intelligence beyond my conscious mind. Experience had taught me to trust myself, so when my head, my heart, and my intuition all gave me a green light to go to Hawaii, I knew it was time to go, even though I didn't know a single person there. I had heard the call to adventure, and I would listen to it.

All the while, I had been writing my first book, a fast-paced science fiction novel inspired by mythology. I'd been working on it part-time for years, and once I finally wrapped up its editing phase, I began to seriously research what it would take for me to spend at least a month in Hawaii, just to get a feel for it. And the more I researched, the more excited I grew. Even though it was technically part of the United States, I got the feeling that, in truth, it was another country altogether, wilder and more raw than any place I'd ever visited. And the beauty and wildlife drew me like no other place ever had.

In my research into how to live cheaply on the islands, I discovered the term *intentional community*, which is a planned community designed from the ground up to have strong social connections and often a high degree of teamwork. I learned that there were many kinds of intentional communities, from ecovillages to retreat centers to co-housing agreements. And they often consisted of like-minded people who held a common vision, such as having a shared diet or meditation practice.

I discovered websites listing intentional communities across the globe, and through those sites I learned that most intentional communities in Hawaii allowed guests for weeks or months at a time. I also learned about work-trade, which is the practice of directly trading one's time for a good or service. In the case of most communities in Hawaii, it meant a shared living space in exchange for a certain number of hours of work per week.

The work-trade opportunities would allow me to stay in Hawaii at a more affordable rate, and with more stability, than anything else I'd seen; and by the time my first book came out in paperback six months later, I had set up an agreement with a community that I felt was a good match for me. And it just so happened to be on the Big Island of Hawaii.

April 19, 2013 was the day my life changed.

With only an Osprey pack and a surge of excitement running through my veins, I watched from my window seat as a barren landscape rushed by, a dark field of jagged, otherworldly rock. Before I could give it another thought, I felt a slight jolt as the aircraft settled onto Kona Airport's only runway, just a few hundred meters from the edge of the island itself. The island looked much drier and rougher than I had imagined, and I was reminded of what I'd read during my research.

An island of contrasts, the west side of the Big Island was dry, but the east side was a true rainforest. The landscape would be greener when I got to the Community in a few days. The photos had assured me of that. What I didn't know, what I couldn't have known, was that I would stay for far longer than the month or two I had planned. I also couldn't have predicted that someone would manifest a blue feather for me out of nowhere, that I would get to hike up to the edge of a molten lake of lava, or that my heart would get swept away.

As we pulled up to the gate, excitement grew within me, and I was immediately struck by how small the Kona Airport was. Across the tarmac, I noticed a small collection of light brown buildings with steep roofs. Then they opened the doors, and we gradually filed out of the aircraft.

I followed a ramp downward, and unlike most people, I wasn't pulling my luggage behind me on a pack with wheels. Instead, I wore my Osprey pack, a rather large but versatile backpacking pack containing everything of value that I owned, and set foot onto the hot dark tarmac, touching the ground for the first time in over five hours.

The warmth of the sun filled my body as I walked, and I took a second to snap a photo of the stunning Boeing 737-800 that I flew in on.

I made my way through the airport, past a rainbow of people, most of whom were sitting on long wooden benches in the gate areas. Thankfully, these were all sheltered from the sun, but the buildings were without walls, allowing a crisp cool breeze to pass over us.

Then I realized: the air. It was different, charged somehow. And it smelled sweet and pristine; the cleanest air I'd ever breathed. It was incredible.

I considered how I was going to get into Kona town. My research had revealed that there was no bus service whatsoever from the airport into town, and the thought of paying $20 for a mere 12 km (8 mi) trip wasn't exactly my first choice.

Back in Wisconsin, I'd read extensively about the culture of the Big Island, doing everything I could to prepare myself for the inevitable culture shock of coming to the most remote population center on the planet.

Despite most people calling it the Big Island, I learned that the true name of the island was Hawai'i (roughly pronounced huh-vai-ee). The comma-like symbol in the name was called an 'okina, and it denoted a brief pause in pronunciation. I would need to keep that in mind since I would soon encounter more of the Hawaiian language than I ever had before.

Most of what I'd read in my research had discussed, or at least touched on, how common and effortless hitchhiking was on the Big Island. I had hitchhiked several times before, so I wasn't too worried as I walked along the shoulder of the airport road toward Mamalahoa highway, a two-lane road that had appeared to be quite hitch-able from the satellite photos I'd studied a few days before.

A row of tall palms lined one side of the pavement, and I walked beside them, noticing the utter absence of a sidewalk. Despite the palm trees, I got the distinct feeling that few people had ever walked along this shoulder, and I felt slightly embarrassed. Still, that walk would be mild compared to some of the things I'd done, and indeed would soon do.

The road stretched on much farther than I'd anticipated, and as I passed the turnoff to the airport parking lot, I stuck out my thumb. Perhaps I could get a ride without walking all the way to the highway. It was worth a try.

Sweat began to form on my forehead, and I wiped it away. All I had to do was reach the highway. Then hitchhiking would be a cakewalk.

Dozens of cars passed me without another thought, and doubt gnawed at me.

No, I had to remain positive. After all, these were mostly tourists, the most wary of all drivers.

A silver car that I'd seen earlier was heading back to the airport but unexpectedly pulled off to the side of the road, pointing toward me. The window slid down, and a man with grey hair called out to me.

"Hey, do you need a ride?" he asked. "I saw you earlier. Where are you going?"

By this point, it had been perhaps a year since I'd last hitchhiked, and with the prospect of a ride so suddenly present, I felt nervous.

"I'm heading into Kona, actually," I said. "Didn't realize this airport road was so long!"

I've long forgotten his exact reply, but as I approached, I got the feeling that he was friendly and trustworthy. When friends ask me about my hitchhiking experiences, I always stress the importance of trusting one's intuition, and I listened to it especially carefully in that situation. Not only was I out of practice, but I was in a different culture.

Soon, I was sitting in the passenger seat with my pack in my lap, a precaution that I usually take when I have valuables inside. We reached the Mamalahoa highway in under a minute, and as we zipped down to Kona town, I learned that the man had worked for Oracle.

He was impressed that I'd made arrangements to work-trade and live at an intentional community without ever having been to the island before, and I told him how I'd felt drawn to the island for years. Something about Hawaii called out to me, and now, with my adventure in full-swing, I felt more assured than ever that I'd made the right decision.

We stopped at a grocery store, and I had my first Hawaii grocery shopping experience. I'd repeatedly read that food was expensive in Hawaii. Some people repeated it like a mantra, but I was prepared for it. Oatmeal was a staple for me, and depending on the brand the price wasn't that much higher than in Wisconsin. Most items weren't as outrageously priced as I had feared, but the price of bananas and oranges was surprising. Bananas were triple the cost I was used to. Maybe a grocery store wasn't the best place to buy them?

I'd been lucky, though. My ride would be passing right by my host's house, where I would stay for two nights. And as we drove back onto Mamalahoa highway, a two-lane route that served as the main loop around the island, I looked forward to meeting Josh, the member of Couchsurfing.com that had accepted my couch surfing request.

I'd long used the hospitality site to find a place to stay during my travels, but I'd found it especially challenging to find a couch to crash on for a few days on the Big Island. People were harder to get in contact with, especially via email. Maybe it was due to the relaxed pace of island life, but when it came to finding a place to stay, I found the lack of response disheartening. Thankfully though, Josh lived in southern Kona and had said that he could host me for a couple nights.

The man dropped me off at a street that led to a small housing development. I thanked him again, and in just five minutes of walking, I recognized the house from the photo on Josh's Couchsurfing profile. It wasn't difficult to spot. After all, there aren't many jeeps that look like they've been owned by Crocodile Dundee.

I walked up to the door and knocked, filled with anticipation.

CHAPTER 2

MAKALAWENA BEACH

When the door opened a few moments later, I was swept up into a house full of busy, buzzing energy. Within minutes of meeting him, Josh regretted to tell me that he wouldn't be around at all during the time he agreed to host me. He and a good friend had decided to hike Waipi'o Valley. Yet he assured me that his mother and brother would be around all weekend, so there wouldn't be any problem.

He gave me a quick tour of the house, which was small with two floors and a cute backyard with clotheslines strung over potted flowers. They even had a little guest room for couch surfers, so I was quite lucky.

Josh excused himself to find some supplies he needed for his hike, and I took that opportunity to get to know his friend a bit. We got on the subject of beaches, and he told me that the best beach on the west side of the island wasn't too far away. All I had to do was hitchhike up to a certain mile marker and take a dirt road toward the ocean. At the end of the road, he said that there was a pristine, white sand beach. Even better, because all the beaches were public property on the island, I could walk along it without worrying about trespassing.

The thought of this heavenly beach filled me with a fresh excitement. I pulled my smaller daypack out of my Osprey pack and loaded it up with a few supplies, put on some swim trunks and a new shirt, and bid Josh and his friend farewell. Soon, I was back beside the highway and stuck out my thumb once more.

Curiously enough, my memory of this hitchhike is fuzzy, probably because my ride and I didn't speak much. Or perhaps I was too caught up in the strange landscape of dark lava fields all around me to notice. We passed the airport road I'd walked down just hours before. Then we passed two tan hills that looked like large breasts, a landmark that would be useful later on.

The driver, an older woman who was concerned for my safety, dropped me off at the mile marker, and I found the unmarked dirt road without too much trouble. I assured her that I'd be fine and began the half-hour trek down the dry, rocky road.

I quickly realized that the road split off at a few points. Josh's friend hadn't mentioned that, and I wasted some time taking a road up a small ridge, only to find myself at a dead end with a stellar view of the ocean in the distance.

After retracing my steps, the road became increasingly rocky and narrow. I passed an empty jeep with a sign apologizing that the jeep had broken down and that the owner would return soon.

Still, the rocky path stretched on, small trees flanking either side. I looked up. Although it was only about 6:00 PM, the sun was nearing the horizon. I'd have to keep an eye on that.

When I reached the water, I found a collection of angular dark rocks interspersed with sand the color of salt and pepper. The waves crashed against them, kicking up the brisk scent of salt into the air, but there was no beach in sight.

I followed the edge of the water past piles of black lava rock, until I came to a few calm pools within the formations, cumulus clouds reflecting on their serene surfaces.

Eventually I came to a wide gate with a sign that warned people not to block the entrance, indicating that it was the caretaker's property. Caretaker of what, I had yet to learn.

There was also a no trespassing sign that had been partially painted over, but as I read it, several people walked around me, ignoring the sign!

Were they locals or tourists? Whoever they were, they had a relaxed attitude toward signage, so I shrugged and followed them through the half open gate and continued following the coast until I saw my first glimpse of white sand farther up.

Then I noticed a pond just to my left that was so dark and green that it drew my eye, sporting layers of lumpy moss and a depth marker planted firmly within the slimy-looking water. It appeared utterly devoid of fish.

I continued around a bend, finding a larger area of white sand interspersed between chunks of black rock. This patch of sand formed a small beach. It was acceptable, but something pushed me onward. After all, the farther I went, the fewer people I saw, and I wanted to see how far I could go. I pressed forward until the sight ahead took my breath away.

Before me was a perfectly pristine patch of white sand, easily the most beautiful spot I'd ever seen in my life. Magnificent cyan waves crashed upon the smooth, luxurious beach, and not a soul was in sight. It was perfection.

I set my daypack down behind a sandy ridge, kicked off my shoes, and ran directly into the waves, letting the warm ocean wrap itself around my body. I had begun my day in the Bay Area, watched California's green coast shrink into the distance, and marveled at the Big Island peaks rising above the clouds during my approach; and now I was here, walking on a pristine beach that felt like it was out of a dream.

As I swam in the ocean for the first time in many years, it finally hit me. I had made it. This was Hawaii. I'd travelled over 6,600 kilometers, and everything had gone smoothly. I was really here, and it was breathtaking.

Now coasting along on an emotional high, I made my first big mistake. I looked around and realized that both my shoes and daypack, with my camera inside, were in plain sight. I decided that, if I wanted to swim without any worry of theft, hiding them would be a good idea. I snapped a few photos before picking up my stuff and finding an ideal spot within the black rocks on the far edge of the beach, where my daypack wouldn't be easily seen.

I surmised that if I walked on the lava rocks very carefully, I would be okay. I tested that idea, and I felt fine. My feet seemed just fine as long as I walked especially carefully. I wasn't going to put my shoes back on until I was done swimming. After all, it would be hard to get them back on with wet feet.

Once I hid my valuables, I felt better and explored the far edge of the beach where some lava rock had formed a beautiful shallow pool that could shield me from the waves. This water was warm too, and I carefully stepped onto the edge and then into the pool. Since the bottom of the pool was sandy, I felt comfortable inside with only bare feet. No one was around, and I closed my eyes, letting the peaceful sound of the crashing waves and the feeling of the warm water soothe my soul after my long journey to reach that singular place.

When I opened my eyes again, I was confused to see something clouding the water. I looked closer and realized that it was blood.

Once I was convinced that it was most definitely my blood and that I had cut myself on the lava rock, I couldn't stop the words, "Stupid, Stupid, Stupid" from looping in my head like a destructive mantra. It was my first day on the island, and I'd already hurt myself.

With greater care than before, I crossed over the black rocks to the beach and examined my feet, finding a gash in the bottom of my foot near my heel. It didn't look deep enough to require stitches, but it was certainly bleeding enough to demand immediate attention. How could I have been so careless to even *attempt* to walk on lava rock? Then again, I'd never encountered such rock before. It was deceptively sharp, but most of the time it didn't hurt to step on it. If I was superstitious, I might have said that the rock had a will of its own, but the likelier possibility was that the danger depended entirely on the angle of pressure and the texture unique to each rock. In any case, I shouldn't have taken the risk. Not out there. Not so far from town, anyway.

By some stroke of luck, I'd brought a paper towel and some food in a plastic bag. Those supplies would be able to sustain me long enough so I could hitch back to Josh's place.

They would have to be.

After thoroughly rinsing the wound with some water I'd brought, I wrapped it in the paper towel and put my foot in the plastic bag. Hopefully, the bag would prevent any blood from leaking into my shoes. I still had a long, rocky trek back to the highway, and the sun was setting faster than I'd ever seen it move before.

Of course. Since I was so close to the equator, dusk and dawn would be shorter here. *"Stupid, Stupid, Stupid..."*

I hobbled back over the black rocks toward the gate with the sign that we'd all ignored earlier, asking everyone I encountered if they were perhaps heading back to the highway. No one was. Thankfully, a few kind people gave me alcohol wipes and a better plastic bag, but no one was heading out.

As I walked, I heard a small squishing sound with each step. I wanted to believe that it was some salt water in the bag making the sound, but I knew better. The wound had bled beyond its wrapping; the bag was slowly filling up with blood, and there wasn't anything I could do about it.

Dusk fell quickly, and after asking a few more people if they were heading back to the highway, I realized that literally everyone still near the beach was camping there for the night. Not only would I have to walk all the way back as the plastic bag filled with blood, but it would be dark before I got there.

I had to get to the highway. If I didn't clean the wound properly and get a real bandage over it, I faced the very real risk of infection.

Pushing these thoughts out of my mind, I plodded along, feeling a sickening squish every time I took a step. Concern swept over me again. What if it got infected? I stopped myself. I'd rinsed the wound thoroughly and cleaned it with an antiseptic wipe. I would be okay. Think positive. It would be fine. Just fine.

A half hour and a world of daylight later, I neared the highway, momentarily excited by a pair of rear lights in the distance. Perhaps they would see my sorry state and save me some walking. In the darkness, I mustered up the energy to run after the vehicle, but it didn't slow down at all, cruising down the rocky road and disappearing down the highway in seconds. All of my running had been in vain, and I took a moment to catch my breath after such a futile dash.

By the time I reached the highway, the stars filled the sky. And with great annoyance at my own bad planning, I stuck out my thumb. I turned up the brightness on my iPod screen and tried to use it to illuminate my outstretched hand, but my little rectangle of light was ignored.

I always disliked hitchhiking at night. Lower visibility makes accidents more likely, and one doesn't get picked up as fast. Then again, I was still new to hitchhiking on the Big Island. Perhaps it was different here.

In a stroke of luck, a sports car zoomed over to the side of the road ahead of me. I'd only been waiting about five minutes alongside an unlit road, a highway no less, and someone had stopped for me. Remarkable.

I approached the car, paying close attention to what my intuition was telling me. Inside the car was a guy who appeared to be in his 20s and seemed friendly. More importantly, it felt right, so I sat down. Most of his dashboard glowed in fine red lights, and the stereo was jamming to island reggae. The guy turned to me and smiled, his dark eyes glinting in the light.

"What's up, brah?"

I hesitated. "Well, I hitchhiked up here, and it got dark faster than I thought it would. I'm staying with a friend in Kona. Where are you headed?"

"I'm headed to Kona." He smiled again and pulled ahead, sending us zooming down the two-lane highway. "I'm Russel. What's your name, brah?"

"Andrew," I said. "This is my first day on the island, actually."

"Hah! Welcome to Hawaii, man!"

Russel drove as if the roads were his own, taking turns at twice the speed I'd consider safe, and the G-forces were palpable. I considered my foot, still bagged inside my shoe. That's all I need, I thought. My heart rate to go up…

The possibility of a blood-soaked shoe flashed into my mind, but I pushed it away. I had to stay positive. As our conversation continued, I learned that he worked at a nearby resort, and I described my destination in more detail to avoid any misunderstandings.

In the night, landmarks zipped past us like specters, and the roads looked unfamiliar to me. I briefly wondered if he misunderstood my directions; yet despite his tendency to drive with the kind of reckless abandon usually reserved for off-road racing, we somehow arrived at my destination unscathed. In fact, I scarcely believed that we arrived as quickly as we did. I'm not sure if it was the blood loss or the jet lag, but if he had told me that he knew a secret route to the south end of Kona, I would have believed him without hesitation.

He zipped up to the house with confidence. "This the place?"

I nodded, noticing the jeep still parked out front.

"Definitely."

I picked up my small brown daypack and waved him farewell, thanking him profusely before waddling back into Josh's house. I followed the familiar stairs up to the living room, calling out to see if anyone was home.

To my surprise, a woman with freckles and a warm smile appeared at the top of the stairs. She introduced herself as Jeanette, Josh's mother.

I explained to her what happened.

"Oh my goodness!" she said. "I'll get you some bandages."

She hurried around and graciously got me bandages and everything I needed to care for the wound, including a hydrogen peroxide sprayer and a towel. Jeanette also gave me a short lecture on the dangers of getting *Staphylococcus aureus*, a bacterial infection that is common everywhere but thrives in tropical environments like Hawaii.

It would not be the last time I got a staph lecture.

I stepped into the bathtub and dismantled my ad-hoc wrapping. My suspicions had proven correct. The bag had torn and blood had oozed into my shoes. I grumbled at the sight and peeled the paper towel off of my foot, causing more blood to ooze out. I sighed, threw the paper and other wrapping into the garbage, and washed off. The bleeding had mostly stopped, and the feeling of the fresh water on my skin felt wonderful.

I rinsed with cold water and sprayed the gash with the hydrogen peroxide bottle Jeanette had given me. The wound stung as it bubbled vigorously, and after a few moments I dried it off with some toilet paper and bandaged it. The wound wasn't as large as I'd imagined, but it was at least three millimeters deep. I'd have to keep an eye on it.

After drying off and getting dressed, I felt reborn.

Jeanette offered me a snack, and we each sat on the bar stools across from the living room, talking up a storm. She apologized that Josh would be gone for the weekend but assured me that she and Josh's brother would be around if I needed anything. She told me how she'd lived near the Rocky Mountains before Hawaii, but once she moved to the islands, she never looked back. We talked well past 9:00 PM, until she said she was getting sleepy.

Was it really that late? The pure excitement of the adventure had filled me with energy, and I didn't feel tired at all. I said good night to Jeanette and picked up one of the books nearby, a blue guidebook called *Hawaii: The Big Island Revealed* that I would later learn was the most famous guidebook on the island, and I read in silence until I heard someone coming up the stairs a short while later.

It was a young woman called Mei. She was a friend of the family and wondered if anyone was around. I told her about Josh's trip and that his mom had already gone to sleep, so we went out to the balcony to talk. She was surprised to hear that I'd come all the way from Wisconsin and shared her love of the islands with me. After talking for a while, she paused and stared at me, sizing me up.

"Would you like to come on a volcano adventure with me? Some friends and I are going out to Kilauea tomorrow. You're welcome to join us."

My eyes widened. I hadn't even been on the island for 24 hours, and I had already been invited to the best island adventure I could imagine.

"Yes!" was my immediate response.

As we talked further, I learned that her friend Ganymede had worked for the US Geological Survey and knew a way to get right up to the edge of Halemaʻumaʻu (pronounced hah-lay-mah-oo-mah-oo), a huge lava caldera within Hawai'i Volcanoes National Park. Basically, we were going to hike up to a lava lake that was right over the Kilauea volcano itself, and later we would all spend the night at her family's one-room cabin in the nearby town of Volcano. (Yes, there's really a town named Volcano.)

Mei warned me that I'd have to get up pretty early. The drive to the southern part of the island would take over an hour, and they wanted time to have a little picnic beforehand. I assured her that wouldn't be a problem and thanked her for inviting me on such a rare adventure.

"No problem," she said. "You seem cool."

I thanked her and said good night, setting my iPod alarm before I passed out. There was no way I would be late for a volcano adventure.

After all, I had wanted to see lava my entire life, and now that dream was about to become reality.

CHAPTER 3

TERRIBLY MAGNIFICENT FIRE

The following morning, I found myself in Mei's car, cruising southbound down Mamalahoa Highway. The sky was crystal blue, with only a few streaks of white in the distance ahead. To our right, the land gently sloped downward, dotted with dry bushes that gave way to black rock and crashing white waves. I had to remind myself that the west side *was* the dry side of the island, after all. The other side would be quite different.

Mei asked me about my adventure so far, and I told her about Makalawena Beach and how I'd cut my foot. She warned me that staph was a serious issue on the island, and I reassured her that I'd cleaned the wound thoroughly and would keep a sharp eye on it.

After a while, Mei said she wanted to stop and stretch, so we pulled off the highway into a tiny overlook area.

As I enjoyed the view of the ocean, Mei propped her leg up on the metal guard rail and leaned into a stretch. In the distance, I could just make out a long pier reaching out into the ocean, broken and worn by years of neglect, and I found it strange that the pier had grown as dark as the lava rock around it.

About an hour later, we reached a section of the island covered in towering white koa trees growing out of a carpet of thick verdant grass. Mei called her friends and confirmed that we'd stop there for lunch. They were only just behind us, so we found a good spot to park beside the koa forest and got out to stretch our legs. Mei took out her hula hoop and played with it, and we talked for a while as we waited.

Her real passion was hula. And with a smile, she told me about how she was going to a circus school on the mainland later in the year. I'd never met someone so serious about hula, and I asked her what she meant by the mainland.

"Oh, that's just what we call the lower 48 states here. Everyone calls it the mainland."

"Hmm. Catchy."

Shortly thereafter, Ganymede and a couple of his friends arrived, and we found a good patch of green grass in the middle of the forest, making our picnic under a shady patch of koa trees. Ganymede was a warm, if rather intense guy, and he picked a good spot for our picnic under the koa trees, spreading out a grey blanket over a surprisingly thick bed of long green grass.

Everyone had brought something to share. Fruit, pad thai, and even poi, a Polynesian food made from the local taro plant that comes in a purplish grey paste. Ganymede urged me to try some, saying that it was traditional Hawaiian food. So I took a bite, a smooth-yet-bitter taste filling my mouth. The aftertaste was slightly sweet, but I didn't especially enjoy it.

I forced myself to try more to be sure. The second bite was even stranger. Not quite bland, not quite bitter.

Nope, not my thing, I thought, and ate some more fruit to wash the bizarre taste out of my mouth.

We packed up our lunch and folded up the blanket, careful to leave no trace of our picnic, and filed back into our two cars. Our next stop was Devil's Throat, a volcanic crater within Hawai'i Volcanoes National Park.

During lunch, I had gotten the impression that Ganymede had learned quite a few of the park's secrets during his time working for the USGS. He told us that Devil's Throat was a uniquely beautiful place. Even better, it was on the way to Halema'uma'u Crater, so why not stop there, too?

Mei and I followed Ganymede's vehicle, taking an increasingly circuitous path until we reached an abandoned parking lot deep within the park. We followed Ganymede down narrow gravel paths, passing by small, mysterious holes that led deep underground, and before long we found ourselves at the lip of a truly massive crater.

I leaned over, snapping a photo of the bottom which was littered with small rocks many meters below. I let my eye follow the rock wall back up to the surface, noting the dozens upon dozens of layers of dark rock, no doubt the result of the many millennia of volcanic eruptions that had formed the island in the first place.

Later, I learned that the crater itself was a relatively modern feature. When Devil's Throat was first discovered in the early 1900s, it was so small that riders on horseback would often jump over the small hole without fear, never knowing that it was over 30 meters deep and becoming much wider the deeper it grew. In fact, it's probably the best example of a collapsed volcanic crater in the world.

We decided to rest beside the crater for a while, eventually lying on our stomachs near the edge, trying to see to the bottom. Ganymede mentioned that we'd need gas masks to be safe at Halemaʻumaʻu and asked Mei if she had any. She did, but they were at her parent's cabin, which meant we would have to zip down to Volcano town to get them.

We drove the short distance east to Volcano, a small town higher up the mountain. Mei's parent's cabin was a charming one-room house just off of the main road that bordered a thick patch of forest. We zipped in, grabbed the masks, and got back on the road to meet our destiny at Halemaʻumaʻu crater.

"In the past, you didn't need any protection to get to the crater," Ganymede explained, "but over the past few years, Mount Kilauea has grown more active. Now the crater releases lots of toxic sulfur dioxide gas. Without masks to filter our air, a simple change of the wind could blow the gas toward us, causing us to choke and vomit from the sulfur dioxide in the air."

The mere thought of that twisted my stomach.

We zoomed back into the park, finding the nondescript parking lot we'd used the first time, and at last began the long hike to the lava lake. Thankfully, the path to the crater was mostly flat, and as the sky grew darker, a strange red glow became obvious in the clouds ahead. I could only guess that we were following an old service road that had been abandoned.

When the road finally ended, it was easy to see the plume of orange and red smoke rising into the sky in the distance. We walked over rough terrain for about another half hour before Ganymede pointed down to something beside some rocks.

"Look! Volcanic glass."

I walked up to him and knelt down, noticing a strange lattice of glass woven over parts of the ground in patches. It reminded me of a spider web, except that it felt prickly to the touch.

"Be careful," Ganymede said, "it can be sharp."

I stood up and surveyed the sky. Once again, night had snuck up on me, and judging from the red glow ahead, the crater was only about 100 meters away. I snapped a picture of the haunting glow before pulling out the gas mask Mei had given me and carefully securing it over my face. Everyone did the same, and we followed Ganymede toward the edge, ever closer.

I noticed some short, wooden pillars nearby. When I asked Ganymede about them, he said there was once an observation post here, but the lava lake had spewed out some huge boulders, destroying it. Ganymede told us not to worry, though. Such an occurrence was extremely rare.

Apprehension filled my heart. Maybe this was crazy. Maybe we should have never come this close. Still, I knew that I couldn't stop there. I couldn't come this far and not stand on the edge of the crater, the caldera.

Soon, I would see Halemaʻumaʻu, home to Pele (pronounced pay-lay), the Hawaiian Goddess of volcanos, not to mention the mythic creator of the Hawaiian Islands themselves.

To many living on Hawaii, Pele's existence isn't a mere legend; it's a reality. For thousands of years, Pele has been honored by the Hawaiians as a powerful being that is meant to be respected, and once we finally reached the edge of the crater, I witnessed that power firsthand.

Below us, a lava lake of terribly magnificent fire seethed with power, its surface roiling in unspeakable patterns which slowly changed as cracks on its surface melted and reformed.

Clearly, Pele is called *ka wahine ʻai honua*, the earth-eating woman, for a reason.

The crater was so large that it was difficult to gauge its size, but later I confirmed that the crater was over 700 meters wide, the equivalent of 14 olympic-sized swimming pools.

An instant later, my skin felt the waves of heat radiating off the lava lake, despite the fact that we were roughly 50 meters above it. The warmth it radiated was palpable, and I found myself unable to look away, consumed by the strange sight of roiling, roaring lava.

That was the last thing that hit me: the sound. At first, the roar reminded me of white noise, but there was something else, a fierceness, like a lion's roar. Except that this lion was much older, much more powerful, and its roar was unending.

I found the sound almost as overpowering as the sight, the heat, and the smell of sulfur. I had made it. I was standing on the edge of a live volcanic crater. At last, after years of dreaming about it, I was seeing lava, an entire lake of it, no less. I took out my camera and shot a few short videos, noticing how bubbles formed and dissolved around the red-hot cracks on the surface.

Never before had I experienced an earthbound phenomenon so mesmerizing. Just a few days before, I hadn't even heard of Pele, but in that moment I wondered if the spirit of Pele might be real, after all.

We stood there for some time, marveling at the destructive beauty of one of the most active volcanos on the planet. I looked over and realized that my companions had long since removed their gas masks and seemed fine. Apparently the winds were in our favor that evening, and after some coaxing, I removed my mask, as well. Then the feeling of warmth on my face grew even more pronounced, the warmth of molten lava.

I closed my eyes for a moment, and it felt almost exactly like the sun on a cloudless summer day.

Ganymede reminded me that we'd brought food. He said we were going to do some extreme picnicking, and I was surprised to realize that I was suddenly famished. We sat down on some of the large rocks that littered the area and pulled out small containers of food. Ganymede had brought beer, and we laughed at the absurdity of where we were eating. Then Ganymede walked over to the edge of the crater and poured some beer out as an offering to Pele, thanking her for letting us stay there for a short time.

As we ate our food, we relished in the incredible experience we were sharing. Someone had even brought wine.

And in the midst of great gratitude toward Mei and our guide Ganymede, we toasted to Pele on the edge of the world.

Once we finished our meal, we began the hike back to the hidden parking lot, following Ganymede down the same service road we'd hiked up earlier, the impenetrable darkness of the forest to either side of us. A sense of awe still filled my heart from the power that I'd seen in the caldera, but as it faded, a vague uneasiness began to settle in my stomach.

To make matters worse, I heard Ganymede and Mei mention something called the night marchers.

"What are the night marchers?" I asked.

Ganymede turned to me, grinning. "The night marchers are Hawaiian warrior spirits, long dead."

"Were they people once? I mean, are they ghosts?"

"I guess you could say that. I've heard that if they find you alone in the forest, hundreds of them will chase after you with spears, screaming battle cries."

A prickly sensation passed over my skin. "Hawaiian warrior ghosts. Sounds like they're pretty unhappy."

"Yeah," he said. "Well, people stole their land."

"Is there anything you can do if you come across them?"

"According to the kahunas," Ganymede continued, "the only thing you can do is strip off all of your clothes and lie face down in the fetal position. That's your only hope for the night marchers to leave you alone."

I paused and considered this for a few moments, imagining what that experience would be like, being so terrified that I was forced to remove all of my clothes and assume the fetal position, on what would most certainly be uneven, sharp terrain.

As we continued down the dark path, images of large ghosts, clad only in loincloths, filled my mind, their mouths open wide with battle cries. I swallowed, trying to settle my imagination. I had never seen a ghost, but if we had seen one fly above us, it would have fit the scene perfectly.

Tiny droplets of rain began to sprinkle down, and I pulled up my raincoat hood.

When we finally reached the car, my pants were halfway soaked, and none of us talked that much on the drive back. There was talk of a hot tub near the cabin, but I felt exhausted.

Back at the cabin, we strung up our wet clothes on a line in front of the wood burning stove in the corner. There was only one bed, which we let the girls use out of courtesy. And before long, I had changed into some pajamas and was lying flat on a sleeping bag on the floor.

I must have fallen asleep quickly, because I have no further memory of that night. I awoke late, just in time to hear that Mei and two of her friends were going into Volcano town to get some food at a local market. They asked me if I needed anything, and I told them that I'd already brought along oatmeal for breakfast. They left soon after, and I enjoyed a refreshing amount of solitude that morning, having a quiet breakfast before heading outside to explore.

The forest outside was thicker than I expected, and I snapped a few pictures of the lovely *Anthurium* blooms that flourished all around the cabin, getting sprinkled on in the process. The sky was overcast, and the clouds continually changed their mind as to whether they were going to rain or not.

When everyone returned from their errands, we packed up our things, careful to leave Mei's cabin in at least as good condition as we found it. The drive back was about two hours, and only later did I realize that Volcano was technically on the east side of the island, not far from where I would be living.

On the drive back, I was delighted to discover that Mei shared my love of singing. Even better, we both enjoyed each other's voice, and the drive back to Kona flew by as we sang classic pop songs from the Beatles and Queen at the top of our lungs. It was a good drive, and as Mei dropped me off at Josh's house once again, I told her how thankful I was for her inviting me on such an unforgettable adventure. Her welcoming spirit would never be forgotten.

Perhaps unsurprisingly, Josh had not yet returned from his hike, and his brother and mother were in and out of the house for most of the day. Still tired from the previous day, I took it easy, eating some food before heading down to their recreational room. An impressive row of beer bottles were arranged on a shelf along the wall, and a dart board had been set up in the corner. I wondered what a party here was like. Probably pretty great.

I looked over and noticed a scuffed up iPod touch lying on a table, mixed in with a bunch of junk. It looked neglected, and I felt sad for the little guy, a useful device left for dead, probably damaged beyond repair.

My mind turned to my next mission: to catch the bus over to the east side in time. The next day I would have to hitchhike to a Kmart about four kilometers north of where I was staying. Not an especially difficult distance to hitch, but the timing might be tricky. Either way, it was going to be a long day.

CHAPTER 4

THE COMMUNITY

The following day was April 22, Earth Day, which felt perfect. After packing up, I bid Jeanette goodbye, walked down the street to Mamalahoa Highway, and stuck out my thumb.

Also known as Route 11, the highway wraps around the entire island and was usually a prime road to hitch from. But since my bus left at 6:45 AM, I was out looking for a ride up to Kmart just after sunrise, a bit early for hitching even on the Big Island. Traffic was understandably light, and as the minutes rolled by, I grew increasingly nervous. I wished that I had just decided to walk, but I was carrying most of what I owned on my back, after all. And no matter how much I tried to get the weight down, it was always a bit heavier than I would have liked, even though I was being as minimalist as possible.

I willed cars to stop for me, but they zoomed past. I checked my iPod. It was 6:25 AM.

Zark!

If I didn't get a ride in the next 10 minutes, I would be screwed. Why hadn't I come out earlier? Hitching had seemed so easy when I first landed on the island. I should have accounted for more buffer time. Oh please, for all that is good in the world, please let someone care. Let someone stop.

To my great relief, someone did, and I arrived at Kmart with time to spare. A small group of people were waiting out front, and I asked someone if they were waiting for the bus. Sure enough, the bus stopped directly in front of the store. Its door folded open, and I paid the bargain price of $2.00 for a 152 kilometer (94 mi) journey that would take me all the way to the Hilo bus station.

This seemed like a crazy deal, but it promoted fewer cars on the road, which is something that the local government was quite interested in. The only downside was that the route, which would have taken two hours in a car, took three hours by bus because of all the stops.

Perhaps that's why the bus was less than half full. Plus, the bus only ran the route twice a day, once at 6:45 AM and once at 4:03 PM. Go figure.

I found an open seat easily, and placed my large Osprey pack beside me, noticing a younger guy sitting on the seat just ahead of me. As we pulled out of the parking lot, he turned around and said hello, asking me about my pack, something about its volume, I think.

"Yeah, it's a 48 liter," I replied. "I've had this pack for over five years. It's served me well."

The young man, called Doran, was full of positive energy, and within minutes I realized that he was probably the most adventurous 18-year-old I'd ever met. He was travelling alone, working on farms, and having a big adventure.

He told me about the culture of the island and how I had to be careful in my decision of where I would stay. Not everyone was friendly, he explained. Some people were kind of crazy.

Oh, how I would come to learn the truth of his words!

After a while, the bus reached the halfway point and stopped to let people have a restroom break. Doran and I got out to stretch our legs by the curb where a small group of people started smoking, and I noticed for the first time that Doran was wearing what I could only describe as air pants. Made of a thin material, the maroon pants moved about of their own accord. And when I asked about them, he said he'd gotten them on the island.

The driver called everyone back onto the bus, and we resumed our trip down to Hilo, enjoying the stunning view along the way.

Never before had I seen a waterfall from a bus window, not to mention stunning green cliffs and ocean vistas. It was easily the most picturesque bus ride I have ever taken in my life. And the entire time, Doran was filling my head with places I had to see, like 'Akaka Falls, Rainbow Falls, Kehena Beach, and Green Sand Beach.

We crossed a final narrow bridge, and the sights of Hilo town filled my eyes. To my right, I noticed that most buildings were only two stories tall, painted in colorful pastels. And to my left, a narrow strip of grass was all that was between us and Hilo Bay.

The bus pulled off of the main road toward a small station close to the bay, and we filed out at the bus station, the main depot for the east side of the island. I checked my phone. My ride was arriving soon, and Doran and I exchanged phone numbers. He seemed sure that we'd see each other again, and I asked if I could snap a photo of him, there at the bus stop. He said sure and gave the camera a nonchalant look.

We bid farewell, and I waited on the curb for Matangi to arrive. Weeks before, she had offered to pick me up at the main Hilo bus station if I did some extra website work for her. I probably wouldn't make such a trade again, but at the time it was worth it for the convenience.

Matangi was the owner of the Community that I would be living in. After extensive research in work-trade options on all eight of the main Hawaiian Islands, her community, nestled in the southeastern corner of the island known as the Puna district, seemed to be the best match for my skills. Basically, they needed a web guy, and I'd been making websites for over 10 years.

Matangi had been quite happy with the work I'd done for her remotely, and I'd built up some time at the Community as payment. I was confident that, with a few weeks to play with, I would have enough time to decide if her community, and the area at large, was a good fit for me.

A large van pulled up, and the window rolled down.

Matangi flashed me a wide grin and confirmed who I was before greeting me warmly, beckoning me inside.

I slid the door open, and once I set my pack down beside me, she and her friend wanted to hear all about how my time on the island had been going.

When I stopped and took stock of everything, I realized that I had only been on the island for three days. In that short time, I had seen more than I expected I would see in a month, and it had been unforgettable.

They asked me if I wanted to stop at a grocery store, and I agreed. I made a quick grocery run, the familiar, air-conditioned setting of a grocery store feeling almost like the mainland for a moment. I grabbed some bananas, oatmeal, beans, tortillas, and such, just enough to get me through the first day or so. Besides, I was pretty tired and didn't want to spend a bunch of time shopping just yet.

Night fell as quickly as ever, the two-lane road lit only intermittently by the highway lights. We passed a familiar sight, a glowing red Longs Drugs sign, before zipping into darkness once again. In an odd way, something about the familiar red logo comforted me. Even in rural Hawaii, there were still elements that were familiar.

We reached a four-way intersection with a stoplight, what I would come to learn was a rare sight in Puna, and continued onward down dimly lit roads. After a while, I was beginning to wonder just how remote the Community was.

Finally, we arrived at the property, and from the forest I heard a strange warbling call radiate out from every direction, almost like birdsong, although something told me that they weren't birds, at all.

It was getting late, and I was eager to set my large Osprey pack down and crash for the night. Matangi and her friend said good night, and to my delight I was greeted by a woman whose smile instantly put me at ease. After an express tour of the property, she showed me to my sleeping quarters, and I passed out in minutes.

The following morning, the sun found a way to stream into my eyes right around sunrise, a trick that Hawaii is a master at pulling off. I got up, changed clothes, and walked over to the kitchen to make some oatmeal for breakfast, admiring the abundant, verdant life all around me. The east side of the island was definitely greener than Kona.

After breakfast, I was given a complete tour of the property, familiarizing myself with some places guests could stay; and I was instantly struck by the exotic flora all around me, learning how to identify the large *Monstera* leaves and many other plants for the first time.

I also met two other volunteers, Wayne and Anne-Marie, that I had a good feeling about almost instantly. They were a cute couple who had been volunteering for a few weeks before I arrived, and they said they were impressed by how positive Matangi had been when she'd spoken about me.

After the tour, we ended up back by the dining area where Matangi and her friend Barb had been talking with another volunteer about eating a healthy diet, and I sat down by the table and greeted them.

Matangi responded in kind before walking off to get something, and Barb said a quick good morning to me before continuing her conversation with the volunteer.

In the intervening years, the specifics of the conversation have left me, but Barb made a point of repeating to the volunteer how hard it was for her to make meals vegetarian.

As I sat across from them, I scratched my head.

"I don't know. I don't find it that hard. When I was first starting out, it wasn't as automatic, but it's not too hard. It's not as strict as being vegan, at least."

Barb grew quiet. "Well, it's different for everyone, you know."

"I guess so. But yeah, if you want any tips… it's really not that hard."

She wore a blank expression. "Thanks."

Hmm.

I wandered off and went exploring, forgetting about the conversation. After all, I'd built up a few weeks of free stay there, and I was going to make the most of it.

I started out easy. I just walked.

When I get to a brand new place, I love to just walk and savor each new perspective. Walking is the speed at which revelations tend to come to me, and I enjoyed my time, passing rows of lush trees, brightly painted houses, and tall grasses. I noticed that a particular kind of tree created a lovely canopy over the road in many places. Dozens of them were aggressively competing for sunlight, and I wondered what species it was.

Even though I was in a rural place, the roads were decent, and I could find my way around without too much trouble. After all, I was not precisely in the middle of nowhere, just in the middle of a jungle that happened to have some paved roads through it.

I returned to the Community and talked with Wayne and Anne-Marie again, learning that they were both a few years younger than I was. This trip was their first time on the Big Island, and they had fallen in love with it so much that they were considering moving there permanently.

They spoke with conviction about synchronicity and strange coincidences, ascribing a kind of magic to the island.

"Manifestation happens a lot faster on this island, Andrew. You'll see."

Little did I know how often their words would come back to me throughout my adventure.

I also asked them about the cooing sound I'd heard the previous night. I had been right; the warbling, unending chorus all around us each night wasn't being made by birds. It was being made by tiny frogs called coqui.

Although I hadn't seen a single frog yet, their cooing call was ever-present each evening, in every tree and every bush, seemingly the voice of the forest itself. And it wasn't until much later that I learned that the frogs didn't belong there at all.

I spent the rest of the afternoon at the Community, talking and taking some photos of the green geckos and red flowers. I quickly learned that the jungle grows improbably fast, needing constant attention to keep it from overtaking sections of the property. I also learned that one volunteer, Greg, was heading to Malama Market later and asked if I'd like a ride.

"What market?"

"Malama. It's a grocery store," Greg said flatly. "I'm heading over if you want to come."

He was very good at saying things flatly without sounding annoyed. If something wasn't interesting, he said it flatly and without hesitation. He was honest and quiet, and I liked that about him.

"You know, I was waiting to stock up until I got to this side of the island, so now is a great time. Thanks, I appreciate it!"

Greg was quiet and smart. Just being around him was usually a calming experience, and he had a few surprises in store for me.

We zoomed into town in his jeep, and I finally got my bearings of the town in the evening light. A while back they had put in a highway bypass so that people could get to the south side of Pahoa without needing to drive through downtown, and we soon passed the four-way stop I'd seen the previous night.

I became absorbed in the sight of downtown Pahoa, internalizing its cozy Main Street, complete with a fuel station, barbershop, Thai restaurant, and an Island Naturals grocery store; and I suspected that each of these places would earn my patronage before my adventure was complete.

We zipped past all of it, until we reached the north end of town, driving into the first mainland-sized parking lot I'd seen since Hilo. Beyond it was the largest building around: Malama Market, its big round sign lit by bright, warm lights. We entered, and the store was pretty typical as grocery stores go, except for the bare concrete floor, which I assumed was a cost-saving measure.

The memory of this visit is significant because it was the first time I really internalized the reality of Hawaii food prices, at least in a grocery store. Milk and animal products were nearly double the price in some cases, which didn't bother me so much since I adhered to a vegetarian diet and am sensitive to lactose.

Once again, the real concern was bananas, which had been over a dollar per pound in every store I'd been in so far. In fact, Malama was pricing them at $1.29 per pound, over twice the price I'd seen for bananas anywhere else in my many travels. (In stark contrast, the price was around 39¢ a pound in Wisconsin at the time.)

Later I would learn that there were more affordable places to get bananas, like farmer's markets. And even at Malama Market, it obviously wasn't going to bankrupt me; it was the *meaning* that I was assigning to the price that bothered me.

On the upside, the employees were warm and friendly, despite the late hour, and I returned to the Community with fresh supplies, itching for a new adventure.

CHAPTER 5

HITCHHIKING TO TACO TUESDAY

Ever since I'd arrived in Puna, I'd heard about a great Taco Tuesday event held every week at a place called Cinderland.

According to the other volunteers, Cinderland was a community relatively nearby. No one I met was exactly sure what time Taco Tuesday started, but the consensus was that it probably began around sunset.

Curiously enough, I have no clear memory the *first* time I hitchhiked in Puna, which is strange because I certainly recall many other firsts. I can only offer one explanation: between settling in at the Community, adjusting to all of the sights and sounds of the rainy side of the island, and meeting so many new people all at once, I wouldn't be surprised if I was experiencing some sensory overload for the first week I was there.

There were a lot of changes to process at once.

In fact, I found hitchhiking to be one of the few things on the Big Island that didn't change much during my time there. It was remarkably reliable, not to mention that it was often great fun; and it didn't take long before I was heading up route 137 to the unmarked gravel road that led to Cinderland.

Thankfully though, my ride was heading directly there. And when we finally reached the gravel road, I looked back to try and attach the turn to some landmark along the highway, but I could discern little in the darkness.

And then I heard the sound of drumming, an unceasing, unrelenting beat that was audible from a long way off as we approached. After a few minutes, I could just make out a hand-painted sign that read: Cinderland Ecovillage.

The driver parked, and I thanked him once again for the ride. He waved to some friends, and just before he disappeared down one of the many narrow paths into the village, he said that I should find him later and offered to take me back to the same spot where he picked me up. I told him that would be excellent, and waved him farewell before walking over to the main sign, which read:

CINDERLAND
ECOVILLAGE
Founded
Feb 17
2000

The drums sounded very close now, and I wandered past the sign and under a towering coconut tree, drawn to the hypnotizing rhythm. The path turned to the left, and I found myself under a huge tarp.

Dozens of people were gathered around a small fire pit, with about a half dozen hammering with great enthusiasm on their drums, ranging from djembe to tabla. They all complemented and supported each other in their own rhythms, moving the crowd into an almost trancelike state as orange firelight danced across their flowing clothes and tanned skin.

Farther down, two bunk beds were set up across from each other, their lower sections repurposed to be comfortable couches that faced one another. Beyond that, a small round table was set in the middle of a kitchen, bustling with activity. A large pot was on the stove at the far end of the covered area, and a huge bowl of salad had been set out next to other smaller bowls. I walked up, and realized that these were all ingredients for the tacos. One man in particular seemed to be in charge, and I turned to him and asked if there was anything I could to do help.

"Sure, you can help chop. But first, hold out your hands."

I looked him up and down. He was taller than I was, and I suddenly felt nervous.

He pulled out a spray bottle. "This is our cleaning spray. It'll disinfect your hands so you can work with the food."

"Oh! Of course."

I held out my hands, and he sprayed them evenly.

"And it's a probiotic," he continued as I rubbed the tangy liquid into my hands, "has some kombucha in it, so it's—"

The drums were too loud, and I missed what he said.

"It's what?" I repeated.

"It's competitive!" He smiled at me, as if he knew a secret.

"Competitive?"

"Yes," he said. "Positive probiotics like those found in kombucha compete with harmful bacteria. Competitive." He nodded, pointing to a stack of bright cilantro on the table behind me. "Go ahead and mince all of that, then let me know."

I nodded, sat down at the last open seat around the small table, and started mincing. Once I was done, he gave me some bright red tomatoes, asking me to dice them and put them in a bowl. And as I worked, other Puna folks, ranging in age from late teens to 30s, sat around the table slicing and dicing.

I smiled to myself. Within 15 minutes of arriving, I had become part of a well-oiled machine, preparing the vegetable portion of what would be our dinner.

We placed the final chopped ingredients in a tidy row on the nearby counter, and I heard someone yell out, "CIRCLE!"

More and more people echoed the word, and the drumming slowed, reduced to one or two people left holding the rhythm. I looked around, unsure of what to do as people joined hands all around me. Someone waved me toward them, holding out their hand to me, and I instantly realized what they meant.

Once everyone had joined the circle, the loop of people extended out of my sight, curving beyond the kitchen, around the fire pit, alongside the bunk beds, before looping back around to the kitchen area. It was a remarkable tapestry of humanity spanning generations, all drawn here for one reason.

By some strange synchronization, about a dozen people began singing at the same time, and I listened with rapt attention. I didn't know at the time that I was hearing a song traditionally sung at Rainbow Gatherings, and I listened carefully as the song continued, spreading around the circle until everyone joined in.

We are circling; Circling together
We are singing; Singing our heart-song
This is family; This is Unity
This is celebration; This is Sacred

We sang it three times before pausing briefly. Then a hum began to spread around the circle, yet this was no ordinary hum. This sound was a long Om, an ancient sound of the universe, used for meditation.

As I joined in, I couldn't help but get caught up in the overtones embedded within our voices. With dozens and dozens of us all contributing our part, there was so much variation, so many intertwining waves buried within the sound, that its beauty stunned me.

The Om ended, and a new quietude spread across the space.

Still holding hands with those next to him, the kitchen director spoke up and welcomed everyone to Taco Tuesday. He thanked us for coming, mentioned that donations of money and time were always welcome, and that they needed servers to dish out food.

In just a few moments, a long line formed in front of the central table, where there was a pot of rice, a pot of beans, assorted toppings, and dozens of freshly-baked flour tortillas forming a little tower on a white plate. I was thankful to already be pretty close to the table and got a good spot in line, taking a deep breath as the drum music resumed its previous energy and optimism. The combination of the sights, smells, and sounds made me feel as if I had left my previous reality altogether, and I hadn't even eaten or drank anything yet!

Once at the table, I received a tortilla piled high with rice, black beans, lettuce, tomato, spicy salsa, and cheese. My mouth watered at the mere sight of it, and the kitchen director was proud to mention that the salsa had some kombucha in it, too. I told him I was excited to try it and hurried over to one of the last open seats on the couch under one of the bunk beds.

The only challenge with sitting under one of the bunk beds was that the lighting was pretty dim, and I often struggled to make out the details of someone's face in the firelight that flickered out from the nearby fire pit.

As far as I can recall, the first person I ever sat by was a teenager, no older than age 17.

Joey was a pretty quiet guy, but eventually he warmed up to some conversation. He hadn't been here that long, a few months. He really liked it in Puna, but he seemed to be on the lookout for somewhere else to stay. Joey asked me where I was staying, and I told him about the Community. He nodded knowingly, and I wasn't sure how to interpret the gesture.

I looked down to my taco, realizing that I hadn't tried it yet, and picked it up with both hands, taking a large bite. Even though the rice itself was a little sticky for my taste, the beans, freshly chopped vegetables, and baked flour tortillas all came together to create a truly delicious combination of flavor.

As I ate, my eyes wandered back up to the fire, and for some time I felt hypnotized by the firelight as it flickered across a sea of faces, all dancing to the unceasing rhythm of the djembe drums. Behind them, a few paths led into the darkness of the forest, and I momentarily wondered just how big this place was before I was distracted by a green beam of light shooting out from the crowd.

I followed the beam of light as it cut through the smoke, my eyes landing on a neon green dot on the tarp far above the fire pit. A laser pointer?

The green dot swirled around in little circles, and I looked back down, trying to find the source of the light, realizing that it was a young boy holding a small device in his hand. He walked toward me, around the fire, and shot the light down onto some drums. His hair was blond, and he wore a bright t-shirt and shorts. He looked to be about age seven or eight, and I got up and walked over to him.

"Aloha! I'm Andrew. What's your name?"

"Kaipo!"

With pride, he showed off his green laser pointer, making tight circles on the wooden floor.

I asked him where he got it, and he proudly said that he got it on sale from Amazon.com. I blinked. Even out here in the middle of nowhere, I still felt the influence of the internet and the global web of commerce.

He darted away, so I walked back to the bunkbeds and leaned on one of the support beams, watching the dancers around the fire before I wandered back into the kitchen to wash my plate. A line had formed in front of the sink, and one of the community volunteers had to repeatedly explain that to start the water, we had to lean on a handle in front of the sink. This device made it possible to turn on the water without using hands, which was pretty cool. Cinderland was a dynamic and fascinating place, and would I have to come back soon.

After I washed my dishes, I got out of line and looked around. The crowd was already beginning to thin out, and I looked over to the fire pit, spotting the guy who had given me a ride earlier. And before long, we were following a dark trail back to the gravel road, the sound of drums fading at our backs.

CHAPTER 6

THE CHICKEN SITUATION

The following morning, the sunlight streamed right into my eyes, waking me up around 6:00 AM. This time I turned over, away from the sun.

When I got up about an hour later, the morning light was still splashed on the green leaves above, and I headed over to the dining area and made my standard breakfast: oatmeal with banana and cinnamon. I don't recall anyone else being around the common area that breakfast, but I didn't mind. Some solitude in the jungle was a welcome change.

As I sat in the dining area, I relished in the abundance of natural light and beauty around me, still marveling that I was, after so many years of imagining it, living on Hawaii, at least for the summer. I still didn't know how this place was going to work out, both the Community and the island at large. Would it be a good fit for me long term? There was only one way to find out.

It had been several days since my foot had been sliced open at Makalawena Beach, and I decided that it was the perfect time to check up on it and redress the wound. I asked Wayne if the Community had anything like a first aid kit, and he was more than happy to help me find some bandages in a nearby drawer.

I thanked him and removed the large bandage over the cut, bracing myself for the sight of blood.

The bandage was predictably red, but the blood was concentrated on one spot. Upon closer examination, the injury was near the side of my sole, a cut less than a centimeter long but deceptively deep. As I washed it off, I got a warning about staph from one of the volunteers. Yes, yes, I knew quite well the dangers of staph. It can get in the blood and really ruin one's year. I reassured them that I would disinfect and be diligent. Thanks for the warning.

This had been at least the third time, possibly the fourth, that I'd been given a short lecture about the dangers of *Staphylococcus aureus* bacteria and its prevalence in that tropical environment. Clearly, it was a big deal.

After redressing my wound, Matangi came up to me, wearing a cold expression. They were planning a trip to the waste transfer station in town, and she must have asked me to get some egg cartons from the kitchen storage area because a minute later, that's what I was searching for. Other volunteers were sorting some glass, but for the life of me, I couldn't find the egg cartons amidst the collection of old pots, kitchen appliances, and stacks of various other odds and ends. Matangi made her way back over to me, saying something like, "What's the problem here?"

"Sorry, Matangi. I can't find it."

She screwed up her expression and knelt down to look.

"Are you blind, Andrew? They're right there!" She extended a finger down to the disorganized collection.

I looked again, speechless.

Her frustration grew, and she screamed at me, right in my face. To the best of my memory, she said something like, "ANDREW, IT'S RIGHT THERE!"

The sight of her angry mouth almost froze me in place, but I turned away, searching frantically for the cartons again.

Finally, I spotted them, a small collection of stacked egg cartons in the midst of the mess. To this day I cannot recall if I ended up grabbing the cartons or if she knelt down and got them first. All I can remember is how stunned I felt that she'd yelled at me so close to my face.

She stormed off, and all I could say was, "Sorry," though I'm not sure she heard me. I sat down and tried to collect myself.

What was going on?

I closed my eyes and took a deep breath. Maybe Matangi was just having a bad day. I had frustrated her. Maybe it was my fault. Had I failed some test?

I walked around to look for Wayne, who I found kneeling over a small patch of flowers and doing some weeding. I told him a bit about what happened.

"She's probably just in a bad mood. Don't worry."

"Yeah," I said. "I just didn't think she'd, you know, yell at me like that."

"Well, she's leaving the island for a few months pretty soon. It'll get better once she goes. You'll see."

I nodded, hoping that he was right.

Later, after she returned from the waste transfer station, I asked if I could speak with her. Matangi agreed, and, feeling that it was best to give her the benefit of the doubt, I apologized that I had trouble finding the cartons earlier. She accepted my apology but told me she was concerned about me.

"I heard about your argument with Barb yesterday," she said. "That's a bad way to start, Andrew."

"There was an argument?" I said, somewhat confused. "We were just talking about food."

"That's not what Barb said. You offended her, and you offended me."

I searched my memory of the conversation. Perhaps I'd come across as conceited? Nothing I had said would offend most people. Yet I had to admit to myself that I'd certainly come across as a know-it-all when I was a teenager. I'd done a lot of self-work since then, but if I was falling back into old habits, it had to stop now.

"I'm sorry," I said. "We had a miscommunication. The last thing I'd want is to offend Barb. I really enjoyed meeting her."

Matangi narrowed her gaze at me. "Very well. Be more careful, then."

Soon after, I found Barb and apologized to her. She accepted my apology and seemed happier afterward. I recall that we even joked around, but as I made my way back up to Pahoa a short time later, my conversation with Matangi lingered in my mind. Something felt off. Then again, miscommunications happen. It's how we work through them that matters.

Hitchhiking up to Pahoa was almost effortless, and I soon reached a white building, tucked just to the side of Main Street with a large sign that read:

ISLAND NATURALS
Market • Deli

To the right of the entrance were two green picnic tables with enough seating for at least a dozen people. Only a few locals were around at the time, and I followed the sloping drive down, past a large palm tree, and up to the door, which slid open automatically. A cool breeze washed over my face, and I smiled at the mild air-conditioning.

For a store with fewer than seven aisles, their bulk section was quite impressive, featuring shredded coconut, fire raisins, macadamia nuts, banana chips, and at least a half dozen varieties of breakfast granola. And that was only the beginning.

The produce section in the southeastern corner of the store was radically different from any store I'd ever seen before. In addition to the standard Cavendish banana that's ubiquitous on the mainland, there were small red bananas and light yellow "ice cream" bananas. There were other strange fruits, too, like bright magenta dragonfruit, whole turmeric root, and carrots in a rainbow of colors. Even better, most of it was grown locally.

I shopped conservatively, grabbing only a few items. I was already seeing ways to stretch my dollar. If I could do that, I might even justify buying some vegan coconut ice cream. It looked incredible, but it was over $8 per pint, a little pricey for me at the time. And at checkout, I used my daypack instead of paper or plastic bags. I noticed that a lot of other people had brought their own bag, too.

To this day, I have continued to use reusable bags when I shop, and I feel good knowing that a small change in my behavior has saved many hundreds of disposable bags from being used once and then thrown away.

After returning to the Community, I cooked a simple dinner of rice and beans, a staple meal throughout much of the world. And as I sat down at the dining area, the memory of my conversation with Matangi returned to me. I brushed it aside, greeting Wayne and Anne-Marie, who were absorbed into watching a TV show on their MacBook.

I sat down across from them. Matangi was probably just having a bad day. Things would improve.

"Oh, that guy's screwed!" Wayne said, pointing to a character on the screen that I couldn't see. A moment later, I heard the character scream, followed by moaning noises.

I looked up to Wayne. "Whatcha watchin'?"

"*The Walking Dead*," he said. "Have you seen it? This season is really good."

"No, I haven't. I'm not much of a horror guy."

He grinned. "Oh, man, it's really good."

"Well, next time I might have to check it out."

Soon after, I slipped off to sleep, surrounded by the cooing sounds of the coqui frogs, intending for a good, peaceful experience on the following day.

The cooing sounds mixed with my dreams, and I drifted away with only a faint sense of the challenges and dangers that were yet to come in my Big Island adventure.

For the next couple days, I focused on getting to know the volunteers at the Community and absorbing as much local knowledge as possible. I kept hearing about Kehena Beach, Kalapana town, the lava fields, and various other landmarks around Puna. One volunteer, Stanley, was an older guy who had rented a car and offered to bring a few of us along on a trip to the Green Sand Beach the following week. Since Green Sand Beach was one of only four truly green beaches on Earth, I jumped at the opportunity. Located at the southern tip of the island, the beach also happens to be near the southernmost point in the US, but it's over two hours down a long road with spotty traffic, so it would be quite difficult to hitchhike to.

Larkin also wanted to come. She was new and had come to the Community for a college project focused on studying different intentional communities on the Big Island to see how they worked. To this end, Larkin was taking a boatload of photos, documenting as much as possible.

Once we solidified our plans to visit the Green Sand Beach, Larkin excused herself and got to work, and I soon found myself in what I can only describe as The Chicken Situation.

Many communities in Puna have feral or semi-feral chickens. On the island, wild jungle fowl are much more common than I ever would have imagined, and before I knew it, one of the volunteers pointed a long BB-gun at one of the older chickens which ran and squawked for its life. Apparently, this particular chicken had become a nuisance, and the order had come from the top: Matangi wanted the chicken summarily dispatched. A wave of excitement washed over the volunteers in the ensuing chase, and I took out my camera to capture some of the mayhem.

The chicken chase was not unlike how I imagine a classic goose chase would be, and when the chicken was at last shot, one of the volunteers grabbed it and cut its head off. (There had been talk of freezing it and cooking it later.)

The volunteer who shot it cut deep into the chicken's chest cavity, pulling out the creature's heart.

I will be the first to admit that I am not a butcher and know little about killing animals, but this seemed gratuitous to me. His feet bare, the man pulled out the heart with his hand and held it up to show us.

If he said anything, I shall never remember his words. The sight drowned them out entirely. The man paused, reaching down to grab his beer with a bloody hand and gulped, smiling over to us. My expression went blank, shocked as he delighted in the destruction of a fellow living creature. I felt that his kill had no honor in it, and the whole situation disturbed me deeply. Perhaps this Community had a sharper edge than even the lava rocks that made up the island. The death here was raw, and I felt ashamed that I'd taken photos of the ordeal in the first place.

Now that it was over, I took a break and reflected on how to best use the rest of my day. Perhaps there was something that could take my mind off of the death that I'd just experienced. What was happening on Fridays? Wasn't there a movie night?

I remembered that a community center in one of the nearby neighborhoods was showing a documentary. If I ate quickly, I could probably hitchhike there in time.

A short time later, I found myself riding on the back of an old truck, racing past a sleepy neighborhood just after sunset. Thankfully, the driver knew about the event and exactly where to drop me off.

I approached the community center, which included a partially outdoor gymnasium that had been converted into a makeshift theater for the night. The only source of light was a white screen a few meters wide that had been set up with rows of folding chairs behind it. I was rather late, and I navigated the shadowy seating situation as quietly as possible, realizing that most of the audience members were quite elderly. In retrospect, this isn't surprising. With its cheap land and excellent climate, Puna is a surprisingly popular retirement destination.

For the life of me, I cannot remember much about the documentary we watched that night. I have tried to recall it at various times, always drawing a blank. Perhaps that is because, compared to what came later, that night was rather quiet, except for one remarkable instance.

As I was leaving, an elderly woman called Elsa asked me how far I had to go to get home.

Perhaps the fact that I was the only person there under the age of 35 tipped her off that I was new. Once Elsa heard that I'd hitchhiked there, she practically insisted that she take me back to the Community, like a grandparent that I didn't want to bother but found myself accepting favors from anyway. I had a distinctly good feeling about her, and accepted her offer.

Elsa had been retired on the Big Island for a while and loved it. I told her that I was about to start writing a sequel to my first book, a science fiction story, and that I also made websites. She was interested in both, and when we arrived at the Community, she told me to look her up when I had the chance. She even made me spell her last name carefully so I could find her in the phone book.

And as I headed back onto the property, I waved back to her with a smile. Then she made a three point turn and disappeared down the road, leaving me in darkness.

I reflected on the day. That woman didn't have to help me, but she did. Perhaps because of the sense of family that pervaded the island, perhaps because I reminded her of someone she cared for, or perhaps merely because she was a selfless person, she'd brought me back to my temporary home at the Community. This act was one of the early instances of the remarkable kindness of some of the Big Island locals.

Such kindness would come to save me in the future, through ways mundane as well as extraordinary.

CHAPTER 7

THE FIRST SUNDAY FUNDAY

On my sixth day living in the Puna district, I headed down to Kehena Beach for the first time. The word on the unevenly paved street was that every Sunday morning there was an excellent drum circle, and my driver knew exactly where it was.

As I soon realized, not only was Kehena the coolest beach around, it was actually the *only* decent beach around. The coastal areas of that part of the island were much younger, geologically, consisting almost entirely of sharp lava rock. Only in a few places had water erosion worn the black rock down to the point of forming small black sand beaches. So while Kehena wasn't technically the only beach in Puna, it had the best mix of accessibility and size, which is probably why it was the most popular. And to make things more interesting, the locals considered it clothing-optional.

We reached a tiny parking area along a low wall and found a spot. I thanked the driver and asked him how I could get down to the beach since we were still pretty far above the water. The driver pointed to a patch of trees, and I followed a few people in, reaching a narrow path that snaked down through boulders and vegetation. Farther down, I saw people turn left and disappear behind more bushes. And in the distance, I clearly heard the beating of drums.

I followed the path down, noticing that it appeared to be deliberately demarcated with stones that had since shifted out of place, resulting in a strange hodgepodge of roots and rocks. As the drums grew louder, I reached a small pool of ocean water that had collected in a shelf of lava rock, and I watched as the waves crashed against the jagged rocks, kicking water up into the pool. I turned, following the path to my left over some more rocks, until I finally stood on a large pile of stones that had been eroded by the waves into round shapes.

Just ahead, a black sand beach dominated my view, so beautiful that I almost forgot about the musical explosion farther upslope. Instead, I just stood there, taking it all in as a half dozen people bobbed up and down with the waves. When a wave hit certain parts of the beach, it pulled in some of the rounded stones, making a soothing tapping sound.

I took a moment to breathe in the beauty of the place.

My gaze was drawn over to where dozens of people were dancing in a circle, playing a variety of instruments. They were having a blast.

Still, I was feeling quiet and waited to approach them, making my way across the beach, up to a small, circular lookout area where a beautiful bouquet of red *Anthurium* flowers had been left out on a small rock altar. Beside them, several cairns had been built, and I paused, photographing the blooms and towers of stacked rocks with the crashing blue waves beyond.

I walked back and sat on one of the logs that formed the back half of the lookout area. It was just past noon, and I took out some food that I'd brought. Even though this place wasn't as mind-blowing as Makalawena Beach, it was still undeniably beautiful, and I closed my eyes and listened to the sounds of the waves. Feeling the waves. Being the waves.

After a while, I wandered over to the drum circle, which was nestled under some tall palms. Dozens of locals slammed out rhythms, with the occasional flutist or guitar player joining in for a time. And there was almost always someone dancing in the middle of the circle. In short, it wasn't much different from Cinderland's drum circle, and I thoroughly enjoyed it. The whole event felt like a celebration of life itself.

When the drumming died down about an hour later, a couple of guys were still wandering around the beach, jamming to their own enjoyment. One was an older man, named Jay, with John Lennon glasses and an acoustic guitar with a rainbow strap. His friend had a silly name: Heartsong.

Heartsong was a big guy with a big heart. Almost everybody knew him or had seen him around, and I got the feeling that most people enjoyed talking to him. On that day, he had a harmonica, and after he and Jay jammed out some tunes, I introduced myself. They were, of course, warm and welcoming. I asked them if I could take their photo while they played, and they said they didn't mind at all.

The rest of my afternoon was spent in the flow, absorbing the waves, music, and community that Kehena Beach had to offer. In fact, the time stamps on my photos indicate that I was there for over five hours. In that time, the only thing that really surprised me was that I only saw one person going nude, which, as I would conclude later on, was preferable.

When I got back to the Community it was pretty late, and only a couple of the volunteers were still awake. Wayne and Anne-Marie had passed out in the common area, adorably still holding hands in their slumber. I smiled to myself as I headed to the restroom to brush my teeth. They were a cool couple, and I was thankful that they were there. Even in those early days at the Community, I felt that I clicked with them more than the others. But what I didn't know back then was just how crucial our friendship would turn out to be.

CHAPTER 8

SOCIAL ABUNDANCE & TRANSIENCE

Two days later, I returned to Cinderland for Taco Tuesday, once again surrounded by a sea of vibrant music and smiling faces lit by firelight. As volunteers helped prepare the tacos, I saw a familiar outline in the group. I approached the small central table and realized that it was Doran!

We hadn't seen each other since our bus ride over to Hilo the previous week, and we were excited to catch up. He had been working at a bed and breakfast in Pahoa town, and when he asked how I was doing, I told him that I was loving the island so far. Most people had been so open and affectionate. I also mentioned the tension between me and Matangi and how she'd yelled at me.

Doran was disappointed to hear this and told me where the bed and breakfast was, just in case I needed another place to stay. They were looking for another work-trader, and if I mentioned Doran's name, they would probably give me a position there.

I thanked him for the thoughtful offer, but I didn't think it was quite so bad as to find a totally new place. Besides, Matangi was leaving for a vacation in under two weeks. Perhaps she was friendlier at a distance. Once I had a meeting with her and got the training out of the way, it wouldn't be so bad.

Doran asked me if I wanted to see more of Cinderland, and I readily agreed. The first time I'd visited, I was hesitant to leave the common area. After all, dozens of people lived there and had their own spaces. The paths had no illumination at night, and I didn't want to accidentally wander into someone's personal space in the darkness. He assured me that people were pretty relaxed at Cinderland, and led me out of the kitchen to a pile of round shapes. Nearby, I saw the sharp end of a machete driven into a log under a tall palm tree.

"It's their coconut chopping area. Pretty cool, huh? If you find one, we can open it up."

I looked around, my eyes adjusting to the darkness. Under the palm tree, there were piles of coconut shells split in two, but no fresh coconuts to be seen. "Maybe later, if I see one. What else did you want to show me?"

He led me around to the left, where a small dorm was. The dorm was completely open to the air with only a large tarp over it, just like the common area. Under the huge tarp, a few structures had been built, a bunk bed, and even a working sink. Most memorable was the elevated wooden floor, which was painted with mesmerizing depictions of goddesses, snakes, and sacred geometry, all swirling in bright colors.

We turned around and he showed me another path that led to the left. There was a smaller building with light inside that he said was the goddess dorm. No one was there, so we wandered back to the kitchen where we mingled some more until the food was ready, hugging people as we met them.

Hugging, as I learned that night, was the default greeting on the island. I didn't need much of an excuse to hug someone, either, and the affection really helped open my heart up. It also felt healing.

One instance really sticks out to me.

Upon introducing myself to one woman, she welcomed me to the village and embraced me tightly. But there was more to it than that. In the midst of the embrace, I felt a profound sense of calmness wash over me, as if her heart was completely open, completely and radically accepting of me.

I thanked her for the hug, and asked her how long she'd been at Cinderland.

"A few months. It's a really special place."

She had a fantastic accent that I guessed was British.

"I love your accent, by the way. Are you from the UK?"

"Yes!" she said. "I'm from England, but I love it here."

Before long, one of the Cinderland organizers called out, "Circle!" and we all joined hands, singing the circling song once more. We hummed Om together, and once again the food was terrific. As we ate, Doran introduced me to more of his friends, a few closer to his own age; and I was struck at the range of ages that congregated there, from age four to over 60. Eventually, Doran and I parted ways, agreeing to hang out at Kehena Beach the following day to catch up in a quieter environment.

I also met Johann around this time, a computer geek who had a warm smile and a gentle heart. He was floating around the island much like Doran and I were, but he implied that he'd made multiple trips to Hawaii over the years. He was passionate about Hawaii, and asked me if I'd ever heard of Harry Jim.

In short, Harry Jim had an impact on Johann in many ways. Apparently, Harry practiced an ancient Hawaiian massage technique called lomilomi. He was also a speaker and educator on Hawaiian traditions and history, and I got the feeling that I was meant to meet him, that it was inevitable that our paths would cross.

As we talked, we headed toward the Cinderland sign, farther from the drums where it was quieter. Johann asked me where I was staying, and I told him about the Community. So far, it was mostly good. And even when I started my volunteer shifts the following week, I would have loads of free time to explore the island. As we talked, I felt more and more that I knew Johann somehow, as if we'd met long ago.

I confessed to him that I was worried about the future and told him about how I suspected that Matangi had anger issues.

I'd observed her anger toward other volunteers, too, and Johann seemed disappointed at the thought. He tried to reassure me, saying that things would get better once she left for vacation. Perhaps we just needed a break. Once I proved myself with good computer work, she would turn around. Johann thought that reading Harry's book would make me feel better. He'd leant his copy to a friend, but once he returned it, Johann would be more than happy to let me borrow it. That plan sounded wonderful. He had spoken of the book so highly that I really looked forward to it. Johann's enthusiasm was contagious.

Instead of feeling nervous about Matangi, I tried to focus on the present moment, and my eyes wandered up to a couple of women swaying around the circle, firelight dancing over their bare arms. There was so much beauty here. How could anyone stay worried for long?

The following day was May Day, and I invited Larkin to come with me for a visit to Kehena Beach. I felt that she would get along with Doran quite well, and I was right. When we reached the coarse, black sand of the beach, he was already there, sitting on a rock. Strangest of all, he was the only one there. We had the entire beach to ourselves.

I greeted him with a hug, and he was really happy to see me. I pointed out something colorful farther up, and we all walked up to the elevated lookout area where the *Anthurium* bouquet had been a few days before. Now there were bigger offerings, with blue and red blankets laid out. New *Anthurium* blooms had been placed in a glass container, and a book was left open at a certain page, held open with rocks. In front of the book there were two antlers. Apparently, some ceremony had taken place here, but no one was around except for the three of us.

We headed back down, and Larkin took off her sandals and pressed her feet into the beach, the black sand contrasting starkly against her light skin. She had questions for Doran, and he was happy to answer them. She seemed impressed at his hitchhiking courage, and as we talked we drew silly faces in the sand. Sometimes I would just stare out into the infinitely blue horizon. It had been so long since I'd lived close to the ocean, and I relished every moment of it.

Doran confessed that he was flying back to the mainland on May 17, and my heart sank. I felt like we were just starting to get to know each other, and he was already leaving in about two weeks. He said he would miss me, and that we should definitely do a lava hike before he left. He would text me. After all, the flowing lava was only a two hour hike from Kalapana Road.

Still, I felt sad. In a way, he felt like a younger brother to me, and I would miss him very much.

I tried to focus on the positive. After all, Larkin and I were heading down to the island's only green sand beach on Saturday. But what would an entire beach of green sand look like? I couldn't wait to find out.

CHAPTER 9

THE GREEN SAND BEACH

The next few days passed in a whirlwind, and I eventually found myself in a sedan heading west with Stanley and Larkin. Stanley was visiting the island alone, and he wanted some travel companions to South Point, a fact that we were grateful for. With smiling faces, Larkin and I watched as the lush green scenery passed by, anticipating the geologic wonder that we were about to see.

Of course, South Point wasn't our first destination. Stanley wanted to be as efficient as possible with his time, and told us that first he wanted to visit Puʻuhonua o Hōnaunau National Historical Park (pooh-oo-ho-noo-ah oh ho-now-now), an ancient place of refuge. Since the park was in Captain Cook, a town clear on the other side of the island, the journey would take over two hours.

Mindful of this, we headed down the ever-present Mamalahoa Highway, passing through the charming town of Naʻālehu (nah ah-lay-hoo), home of the southernmost *anything* in the USA. There aren't any towns south of there, so it's pretty easy to get "southernmost" as part of one's business title.

We didn't have time to explore the town that day, which was for the best because I would spend considerable time there the following year.

After a good long while, we finally reached the park, which was nestled within a small peninsula on the coast. A sign at the entrance read:

Because this area is considered sacred.
No picnicking, smoking, or sunbathing please.

That was understandable, considering that it was no ordinary national park. In truth, it was a sanctuary. We read more about the place, learning about its rich history. In centuries past, any fugitive who had broken Hawaiian law could seek refuge and forgiveness within the walls of Puʻuhonua. Even in the event of war, families could seek refuge within its walls and be assured to return home safely, regardless of the outcome.

Truly, it was a sacred place. Stanley said that we wouldn't stay for long, just enough time to explore a bit; and we wandered in, soon reaching a small bay bordered by salt and pepper sand.

Through a patch of short palms in the distance, I could see a group of people moving in a synchronized motion, all dressed in matching blue shirts.

We grew closer, following the beach around to a large sandy area where about 20 people were performing a carefully choreographed dance. They appeared to be in their 20s and 30s and represented all shades of the human rainbow. Together, they put one foot out and two hands forward. Then they all turned, stretching out their right hand and then their left. I had stumbled upon a live hula performance!

I smiled as I watched the group tell a story with each wave of their hands. The performance calmed me, and I felt so grateful to finally witness hula, a dance form originally developed on these islands long ago.

And before I knew it, the dance ended. I had only been watching for about two minutes and felt sad that it was over. Then I realized that it was great luck to stumble upon a hula performance in the first place, even if I only saw part of it.

We wandered back over toward the water, where I noticed beautiful wooden figures, carved out of whole trees. Some were fierce with mouths open and nostrils flaring, and some were more stoic with long, contemplative faces. As I looked at them, the ancient figures filled me with a strange sense of longing, although I couldn't pinpoint exactly what I was longing for.

We each wandered off in different directions, and I followed the path across uneven lava rock that bordered the ocean, over to a truly massive boulder, almost as tall as I was. A sign nearby explained that the ali'i (pronounced ah-lee-ee), the Hawaiian chiefs of old, would sit on this rock to relax, and implied that it was fine for me to do the same. So after some careful climbing, I sat down on it.

From the top of the boulder, I got a better view of the low rock walls around me, but the stone's surface felt awkward. Perhaps the chiefs had some padding that they would bring with them? Still, the view of the ocean was soothing, and for a moment, I allowed myself to imagine what it would be like to be an ancient chief, confronted with the challenges of leading my tribe, looking out onto the black lava rock and the crashing ocean beyond and perhaps finding some solace in the waves.

I jumped down and followed the trail around, reaching a place where high black walls had been carefully built out of lava rock. Despite the uneven shape of the stones, the walls were incredibly straight, revealing the profound skill of the ancient Hawaiians. Somehow, they could even make a wall feel magical. Later, I found out that this was called the Great Wall, one of the boundaries of the place of refuge.

Farther down, I met up with Stanley and Larkin again, near a huge hale (pronounced ha-lay) at least two stories tall without any front or back walls. Today, we might call it an A-frame, and inside there were two handmade canoes, beautiful examples of Hawaiian craftsmanship.

We'd already been there for about an hour, enough time to see the highlights of the park. But at that rate, we wouldn't reach

South Point until 3:00 PM, so we had to get moving. Stanley asked us if we were ready to go, and we all agreed.

Once again we cruised down Route 11, the clouds gathering above us, yet it didn't rain. We were on the dry side of the island, after all. It didn't rain here every day like it did in Hilo.

After about an hour, we finally made the turn onto South Point Road which led down to the southernmost point on the island, and consequently the southernmost point in the entire United States.

Yet, the road didn't quite reach all the way to the green sand beach. The terrain became too rough and gave way to a rolling, sandy landscape that only four-wheel drive vehicles could handle. And even if one had a capable vehicle, it would probably be worse for wear after heading down one of the dusty dirt roads that crisscrossed the southern tip of the island.

As we headed down the narrow road, the coastal cliffs became clearer. In the distance I saw a row of 14 wind turbines, a smart use of the space considering that South Point is almost always windy. Later, I learned that it was the Pakini Nui Wind Farm. Completed in 2007, the wind farm can supply a maximum of 20.5 megawatts per year to the island's power grid. (And yes, it is the southernmost wind farm in the United States.)

The vegetation grew sparse, until only grassy ranges were left. We reached a fork in the road and saw more evidence of the wind. Every tree and bush that peppered the grassy open range had been visibly windswept to the west, like a hairdo created from sticking one's head out of a car window.

We turned toward Green Sands and eventually pulled up to a dusty parking lot where a few beat up old trucks were parked. Signs warned that travellers would need four-wheel drive to continue. Then I noticed that a bunch of people were exploring a sheer cliff nearby, and with great excitement, we jumped out of the car.

When I reached the cliff edge, I was shocked at how many shades of blue mingled in the water. Caribbean blues danced with indigo and sapphire tones. Farther down, there were rock formations forming little plateaus just above the water that led into tiny caves, and I relished in photographing it all.

Someone nearby took a running jump off the cliff and plummeted down into the water dozens of meters below, making a huge splash. Laughing, they swam over to an iron ladder that led back up to the top. Stanley said that he was going to jump, and Larkin said she would, too.

I wished that I'd brought my swimsuit.

Or perhaps I'd left it on purpose. At that point, I wasn't sure. Because my eyes were pretty myopic, I was hesitant to swim in the ocean without my glasses. Imagine swimming in a blurry blue mass and having to find a faint blurry outline of a ladder in the distance. It's not fun.

Stanley jumped off the cliff with gusto, hitting the water like a cannonball.

Why didn't I bring my contact lenses? Was I out of them? I cannot recall my reasoning at the time, but I know that there were multiple factors for why I decided not to swim that day. Perhaps I was strange, but my interest in the nearby Green Sand Beach was not to swim there. My interest was to simply see it, to photograph it and marvel at its unique beauty.

Larkin asked me if I would take a photo of her jumping off the edge, and I told her that I'd be happy to, setting my Fujifilm camera to burst mode.

"Okay. Ready?"

She backed up and made a running jump off the cliff, and I pressed the shutter as she careened through the air, releasing the button the instant she hit the water. Nailed it.

As Larkin swam over to the iron ladder that led back up, I noticed that Stanley was wearing snorkeling gear as he swam in the sapphire water far below. Shortly after, he climbed back up and asked if I would photograph him jumping off the cliff, too.

"Of course." I backed up to frame the shot. "Ready?"

To my delight, I managed to capture a photo the instant he hit the water. Two for two.

After a brief exploration of a rock formation that let ocean water into a dangerous pool nearby, we discussed our options to reach the Green Sand Beach. We could either walk the trail, which was just over 1.5 kilometers (about a mile) or we could pay one of the small, and surely entirely cash-based, businesses in the parking lot to take us down on one of their pickup trucks. I voted to walk. It wasn't that far, and we could see more along the way.

I lost the vote two to one, and we found ourselves negotiating with one of the drivers, who quoted us something like $10 per person for the short drive. I almost laughed at the price, and we continued to negotiate. Eventually, we got him down to $20 for all three of us.

I turned to Stanley, feeling guilty that I had no paper currency, just a card.

"I don't have any cash on me. Can I pay you later?"

He said something to the effect of, "Don't worry about it."

The only problem was that there was only room for two people in the truck. Since Stanley was the eldest and I didn't want Larkin to have to choke on dust on the way down, I elected to take the flatbed, sharing space with a spare wheel and a cooler. I'd be fine, and it might even let me take better photos.

The truck roared to life, and we zipped over the sandy orange landscape, passing dozens of people who had decided to walk. Unfortunately, the truck also kicked up a great deal of dust, and I felt vaguely guilty that we were disturbing their otherwise peaceful hike.

The rolling dirt road was so windy and weird that it took us about 15 minutes to reach our destination, but when we at last arrived, the sight left me speechless.

Just beyond a low rock wall, the ground sloped down at almost a 45 degree angle until it met with a narrow bay far below. On the right, the bay was shielded by a dark wall of rock that extended out into the ocean, and a narrow path snaked through the rock formations and led all the way down to the sacred beach. From that vantage point, it was a muddier green than I'd imagined, but it was still a remarkable sight.

My eyes followed the beach back up to the left, where an otherworldly rock formation rose into the sky, strange wavy patterns stacked one on top of each other. Later I learned it was Puʻu Mahana, an ancient cinder cone that had eroded and made up the long eastern wall of the bay. According to the USGS website, the cinder cone, whose name means "warm hill" in Hawaiian, formed over 49,000 years ago, which isn't at all surprising given the hundreds of layers I could see as they slowly eroded into the sea.

Between Puʻu Mahana to my left and the dark wall of lava rock to my right, sea-green waves lapped up against a long strip of olive sand. I was finally here, at Mahana Beach, one of only four true green sand beaches on Earth, and it was magnificent.

We split up, and I just stood at the vantage point for a while, photographing that singular perspective before starting down the narrow path that cut through the rock and down to the beach. When I looked back, I noticed that I'd been standing on a shelf pointing slightly upward, formed by stacked layers of rock. My eye followed the layers, and I realized that they were part of the same structure as Puʻu Mahana, the eroded cinder cone that bordered the bay. Everything was connected here.

A new urgency came over me, and I followed the narrow path that snaked through the rock formations until I finally reached the beach itself.

To be honest, I was disappointed at first. Up close, the beach was less green and more brown than I had expected. At least, it wasn't any shade of green that I had seen before.

Had I missed something?

I crouched down and examined the sand, realizing for the first time the rainbow of color buried within it. At certain angles, the sand did indeed sparkle in green. I took a handful of sand and studied it closely, realizing that there were grains of almost every color: white, brown, olive, yellow, black, and even red. I stood up, taking care to notice how the colors mixed together. Most of the grains were either black or greenish.

Later, I learned that the green particles were olivine, a mineral that was found in high concentration in the magma that created the nearby Puʻu Mahana cinder cone. As the cone eroded, lots of olivine was released, causing the beach to grow over time. And because olivine is denser than most of the other volcanic particles eroding from the cone, it tends to stick around, accumulating over time until it eventually created the beach.

Something up on the surf caught my eye, and I looked up. Some people were catching a few short waves on their bodyboards, and I whipped my camera up and snapped three photos in quick succession as a surfer rode over a wave, arms outstretched in joy.

Mahana Beach truly was a magical place, and I took some time to try and capture the beauty with my camera, noticing how the black rocks on the west side of the bay provided some stunning contrast against the blues of the ocean and the dark green of the beach. People in blue, green, and yellow swimsuits frolicked in the water, and I did my best to avoid getting them in the picture, at least for the landscape shots.

Nearby, I came across three kids who were enjoying themselves with the ancient pastime of digging a hole in the sand. Inside, I could see the white grains in the sand glisten, almost as if they were glowing in the dark.

The olivine sand was better sandcastle material than the black sand of Kehena, and the kids had made a rounded dome similar to the ones that I'd made as a kid.

After a while, I got the feeling that Stanley was almost ready to go. It was late afternoon, and it would take us about two hours to get back to the Community. After asking someone to photograph me in front of the beach, I took the narrow path back up. On the way, I passed a sign that said:

Welcome to Mahana Bay
Please do not take sand or graffiti on the walls.
Mahalo, The Locals

Stanley called down to me, and I walked faster.

Soon, we were all back in the rusty pickup truck, and I took one final look at the geologic miracle that was Mahana Beach. And then the truck whisked us away, kicking up a new storm of orange dust.

On the drive back, I reviewed the photos I'd taken and let Stanley copy them from my camera to his iPad using a clever adapter he had. I'd caught the bodyboarder at the perfect moment, just when he'd hit the apex of the wave, ocean spray behind him. That's what visiting Green Sands felt like. Every moment felt like the perfect moment, and I felt so grateful to have had the opportunity to see it. When we got back, Larkin and I thanked Stanley profusely. He only smiled.

CHAPTER 10

A NIGHT HIKE ON THE LAVA FIELD

The following day was Cinco de Mayo, and I headed up to Maku'u market for the first time. I was surprised to see that the Sunday market was big enough to have its own parking attendant, which is saying something in Puna. It was easy to get lost in the dozens upon dozens of stands. And as I browsed the various vegetables, fresh coconuts, hot lunches, and jewelry for sale, live marimba music soothed my senses.

The variety of items available at the market bordered on the bizarre. There was even a hot water heater for sale, and for some reason, an old toilet had been cleaned up and converted into a rather hilarious planter, sprouting bunches of orange flowers out of its bowl.

When we got back to the Community, dinner preparations began, even though it was only late afternoon.

I cannot recall whether or not the idea sprang from a direct observation of the Battle of Puebla or just the fact that it was a Sunday, but we all took turns in the kitchen making a little something for a Cinco de Mayo dinner.

That evening, I enjoyed watching Greg show off his culinary skills, his body like a force of nature moving from place to place as he used all of the counter space and stovetops we had available to make a delicious main course. Fresh onions, coconut milk, lemon, tofu, rice, carrots, and so much more came together to make a truly delicious dish that was similar to yellow curry.

Even so, my thoughts were drawn to the next day. My friend Doran, young adventurer extraordinaire, had invited me to go on a lava hike the following afternoon. He would be leaving the island in less than two weeks, so I was thankful that he had found time to take me and another friend of his out onto the Kalapana lava fields. Of course, I had already seen lava at Halemaʻumaʻu, but I had been standing on a cliff, dozens of meters above it. On the Kalapana lava fields, there was a chance that I could get much closer than ever before.

That night, we had a wonderful Cinco de Mayo dinner, but even as I ate, I couldn't get my mind off of the lava hike Doran and I had planned for the following day.

Soon, I would see lava up close.

All the while, I felt the concept of "island time" begin to seep into me. Days seemed to move faster, and it was more difficult to tell how long I'd been on the island. So much had been happening, and the weather never changed. Usually it would rain at night and be sunny in the morning, followed by rain for perhaps an hour in the afternoon. It varied somewhat, but after a while, I began to see how someone could really lose track of the months, even the years, here. Something about the place affected my memory in unpredictable ways.

Perhaps that is why, for the life of me, I cannot remember how we got to the small parking lot on the border of Kalapana. Doran's friend must have had a car because I clearly remember parking there and walking past a small, white booth on the way to the lava field.

As we passed, a man in the booth asked us if we were interested in lava boat tours, so I stopped and looked at his pamphlets. For something like $100 per person, his company would take us out on their boat for a few hours to see the lava spill over the Kalapana cliffs into the ocean, creating a stunning sight and usually plenty of lava haze.

It was a hot business idea, until the lava stopped spilling into the ocean, at least.

I smiled and thanked him for the offer. But Doran and I had a more pressing need. Since it would take at least two hours of hiking across the uneven lava rock to reach the hot spot, we had to move quickly if we were going get back before it got too late.

Although, I didn't know it at the time, our hike took us across the East Rift Zone, downslope of the lava lake that I'd seen a few weeks before. In addition to Halemaʻumaʻu, another volcanic cone called Puʻu ʻŌʻō had broken out and had been erupting continuously for 30 years at that point, making it the longest-lived rift zone eruption of the last 200 years. The flow was unpredictable, but all we had to do was find a single glowing spot, where the flow reached the surface.

We followed the gravel path up to a large black mound that functioned as a lookout point for the lava field. My eyes scanned the unending field of otherworldly black rock, devoid of any trees or discernible vegetation.

I turned to Doran. "Shouldn't we see the glow of the lava on the horizon? You're sure it's on the surface?"

"Dude, I was just out here like last week. It's still going. It's about a two hour hike, but you'll see it once we get closer."

"Okay." I smiled. "Thanks again for being our tour guide today. I really appreciate you taking me out here."

He grinned back at me. "Of course. A friend took me out here the first time, so I want to pay it forward."

We walked off the black mound and down onto the lava field, pressing predominately westward across an utterly barren, charcoal landscape that stretched out into the horizon.

Well, not quite. As we negotiated the sharp, rolling bulges of lava rock, I noticed small green leaves reaching up from the cracks in the rock. Even in an environment totally without soil, certain plant species had adapted to take root on the lava rock itself. And, as I learned later, plants like those were the first to colonize the island after it rose from the sea, eons ago.

The next hour was pretty quiet. We passed another group heading out, taking a slightly different route westward. Their slight difference in trajectory became more pronounced over time, until they vanished behind a lava mound. Like razor sharp hills, the landscape was littered with these mounds, most over seven meters wide. If they weren't so angular, we might have walked right over them, but it was actually much easier to walk around them. As a result, it was impossible to take a straight path westward. It simply wasn't something the lava was going to allow us to do.

And so, we followed a curving path around uncounted lava mounds and wide cracks in the landscape, all the while noticing the sinking sun ahead of us, until it at last dipped below the horizon. The dusk quickly turned to night, and the new darkness revealed a glow ahead that we hadn't noticed before.

We switched on our flashlights and pressed onward, excitement bubbling up within us. Several points of bright, red-orange light emanated from far up ahead, and we headed toward the nearest one. All the while, I had to be careful not to make a false step on the uneven rock as I snapped a few photos of what was surely lava light.

Walking on lava rock at night is tricky, even when one has a light, and we had to continually examine the path ahead with our flashlights to avoid twisting an ankle or getting cut on the sharp edges protruding from the ground. We also found it difficult to judge distance, and for the next hour, the dots of light didn't seem to grow that much.

Then we lost sight of the light altogether, until the ground inclined upward slightly, as it often did, and from this higher viewpoint we finally saw it: a wide, gaping wound in the landscape, glowing in bright red.

Even though we were many meters away, I could already feel the unmistakable heat of the lava on my face, and as we grew closer, I had trouble taking my eyes off of the thick, red material. From our new vantage point, I realized that the lava was flowing just under the surface of the ground up ahead, and what we were seeing was the brief section where it was exposed to the air, before sinking back under the hardened lava rock once again. And all around the open wound, a thin spider web of lava light bled through cracks in the rock.

The sight was mesmerizing, and I tried, mostly in vain, to capture the fierce beauty of what I was seeing with my camera. Yet the lava was so bright compared to our dark surroundings that it overwhelmed my camera's sensor for most of the shots, creating purple halos in my photos. Eventually, I put my camera away, struggling with the question of how close I should get. We were perhaps seven meters away, and my face was already sweating from the intense heat.

Doran wanted to stay on the safe side, but I wanted to move closer to take better photos. Whenever I zoomed, I lost too much light. Getting closer would fix that, but Doran warned me that the lava rock might be thin at any point. If I got too close, the rock could potentially collapse under me, and I could lose a limb, or worse.

We stood at a safe distance for some time, watching the lava curl in on itself in ever stranger formations. Oddly, the smell of sulfur was mild compared to what I'd smelled at the Halema'uma'u caldera.

Doran told me that sometimes people *could* get closer, under the right conditions. It all had to do with the temperature gradient beneath our feet. If it was shallow, it was difficult to get close to the lava without burning one's arms and face, but if it was a steep gradient, one could get quite close without burning oneself. He'd even heard of people roasting marshmallows over the lava and eating them. Later, I did some research and found a video of locals doing just that.

I checked my iPod. It was nearly midnight, and I asked Doran if we should start heading back. He pointed out the glow of lava light up by the coast in the distance, and we agreed to check that out first. The boat companies were selling tickets to an oceanside lava tour, after all.

We trampled over more of the wild lava rock until the smell of sulfur grew stronger than before, and Doran abruptly stopped walking. The intensity of the smell made him uneasy, and he didn't want to continue. I checked the wind, and it wasn't blowing from the glowing area where the lava was. I felt that we would be okay, but he didn't want to risk it.

We turned around and headed back in the direction we came from. Something about this new leg of our hike made me nervous, and after some minutes of walking it hit me: the parking lot had no light. We were heading toward a pitch black nothingness, our memory as our only guide.

At first, we tried to gauge our direction from a point of light on the ridge that had been on our righthand side when we'd hiked out. This idea proved helpful but still imprecise in our quest to find the parking lot, and for over an hour we scrambled over lava, heading vaguely east as we tried to find our way.

Another hour passed, and we reached a jagged incline of rock which I climbed to get a better view, hoping it would provide us with a better idea of where we were.

To my shock, the incline dropped off to a sharp cliff, and when I flashed my light ahead, I could see the tops of trees just below. Had we really gained that much elevation?

A sense of dread began to creep up on us as we struggled to find our direction in the night, feeling more and more like fools that none of us had a device with a GPS chip. If ever there was a dire need for GPS, it was on that night.

On a whim, we headed north, realizing from the cliff we'd discovered that we must be south of where we started out. The trees must have been growing in a collapsed lava tube that had created a depression in the land. If we headed north for a while, we could swing around the lava crater and then head east, back to where we'd come from.

But as we headed north, we saw a strange sight far ahead: a series of tiny white dots of light, floating over the darkness of the lava field. Exactly how far they were was difficult to determine because they were only points of light, totally without dimension.

We pressed on, ever watching the white dots in our peripheral vision as we headed roughly northeast, and after a while, the position of the dots grew clearer to us.

The sight made me stop dead in my tracks. "Guys, do you see that? They're in a perfect circle. Are you seeing what I'm seeing?"

Doran was silent for a moment, measuring his words. "Yeah, I see it."

"What do you think it is?" I said, my eyes trained on the strange circle of lights that simply should not have been there.

He seemed unsure of how to respond.

"I don't know," he said. "But we need to keep moving."

As we walked, my eyes darted back to the circle of lights periodically. Every time I moved, they shifted. I tried to calm myself down, tried to tell myself that they were only shifting because our perspective was changing.

Then I saw something that took my breath away. Some of the lights in the circle moved up and down slightly in a way that almost seemed rhythmic.

"Did you just see that?" I said. "It looked like they moved!"

We all gazed out onto the points of light, which now appeared to be in a slightly different circular configuration.

"I swear I just saw it move," I said, trying to push down the fear growing within me. But I couldn't deny what it looked like. "Doran, that's a clear saucer shape. What if it's—"

"Dude, chill out!" Doran said. "We just need to keep moving. I don't think it's dangerous."

Eventually, the lava rock leveled out more. Still, the circle of lights loomed ahead, almost menacing in their presence, and as we pressed on, the contours of the land itself seemed to nudge us closer to the lights, even though they were north of us, and we were trying to head northeast.

Then, somehow, our feet found a gravel road. I looked down to the rusty gravel and breathed a sigh of relief.

"We should follow this road to the lights," I said with conviction. "I for one am not going to go my entire life without knowing what we really saw tonight. I have to know."

Doran and his friend nodded in agreement, and we followed the gravel road up, until the circle of lights did something quite un-circle-like: it broke up.

"Okay," I told myself, "so our perspective changed again. Maybe it's not a circle at all, but I still need to know what these lights actually are."

We walked along the gravel road, heading toward the nearest light. What *was* this strange source of white light in the middle of the Kalapana lava field? My pace quickened as the light took on more and more dimension.

And then, I saw the light for what it was.

I blinked at the odd realization that, for the entire time, I had been looking at an LED light near someone's garden.

Of course! We were in the residential development, built on top of the lava, called Kalapana Gardens. I'd heard about this place, and I could just make out the outlines of other houses, blocking out parts of the starry sky, all around us.

But what about the other lights? I whipped my head around, taking in my surroundings from my new perspective.

Dotting many of the houses around us were similar white LED lights, and my eyes were opened.

"They were *yard lights* this whole time?" I said, bewilderment washing over me.

"I guess so."

"Wow," I whispered, finally letting myself relax. "Perspective really is everything."

Ahead, we heard footsteps, and I tensed up again.

"Hello?" I said. "Who is that?"

We shined our flashlights ahead, seeing an old man approach.

"What the heck do you think you're doing out here at this hour?" the man called out.

We apologized, explaining that we had hiked out to see the lava and gotten lost.

"Will this road take us back to the main one?" I asked.

The man grumbled in annoyance. "Yeah. Just follow this up. And try to be quiet. People are sleeping."

He lumbered off, and I wondered how loud we'd been.

I turned to Doran. "Were we being loud?"

"I don't think so. We were just talking."

I wondered how well our voices travelled over the lava at night. The wind was loud enough. More likely, the man had seen our flashlight and grown suspicious.

We followed the narrow gravel road to an open gate that led to an intersection. "Left or right?"

I looked up to the bright light on the ridge that had served as our guide. It was directly ahead, so we were pointed roughly north. "I think right."

"Me, too," Doran said.

We followed the gravel road until we saw the familiar warning sign just before the lava field began. And after over five hours on the field, we set foot on solid, paved road once again.

Minutes later, we reached the small parking lot and found the car. With great relief, we piled in, the soft padding of the seats a welcome feeling against our sore bodies.

I cannot even recall returning to the Community that night.

CHAPTER 11

THE MEETING & INTEGRATION

Several days later, Matangi and I had a meeting about my future at the Community. It had been some time since I'd spoken to her one-on-one, and I felt a bit nervous. Thankfully, she seemed to be in a good mood that day, so I went into the meeting feeling confident, or at least, doing my best to project confidence.

We met on the outdoor patio, and she asked me how I felt things were going. I told her that I enjoyed life at the Community. They had a diverse group of volunteers, and I would be more than happy to work-trade there for a while. She said that she was happy with my work, but she had reservations.

"You really need to pay attention to people's body language, especially in group settings. Just because someone is having a conversation in the same room doesn't mean you can add your two cents. I've observed you doing that several times, and not everyone likes that, Andrew." She smirked at me.

"I'm sorry," I said. "I'll definitely be more sensitive to that. To be honest, I'm still adjusting to the island, and sometimes I feel overwhelmed. I've also never lived in a community of unrelated people like this before, but I'll do everything I can to be more aware of people's body language in the future. It's important to me to be a positive part of this community."

"Good." She pulled out her phone and was silent for a few moments. "Okay, how about we have you start your volunteer schedule this Saturday?"

I winced slightly. "I'm sorry, maybe I misunderstood. Because of all the website work that I did remotely, I built up three weeks of stay here, right? That means my first work day wouldn't be until Monday, correct?"

Matangi explained that they really needed someone to cover on weekends and gave me the feeling that I would be sorry if I debated her on that point.

"All right." I shrugged. "It's not a big deal, anyway. Just a minor scheduling shift."

I said this to her, knowing in my heart that she was not entirely holding up her end of our agreement, but I tried not to focus on it.

She flashed a smile at me. "Just remember, you'll do fine as long as you remain humble and don't overanalyze. Especially if, going forward, you don't butt into people's conversations."

I scanned my mind for an instance where I'd butted into someone else's conversation, and all I could come up with was the original conversation with Barb. Was she still holding onto that? After all, I'd apologized. We'd had a good talk afterward, and I'd had only positive interactions with her since then.

I inhaled slowly.

"Of course," I nodded. "Like I said, being a positive part of this community is important to me."

Matangi excused herself for a minute and returned with a short contract for me to sign, which I read carefully. It protected the Community from a lawsuit if I got injured on the property and required that I give plenty of notice before I moved on from my volunteer position, which was unpaid. Even so, it was understandable. Matangi needed to be sure that the positions would be filled while she was away.

Nothing in it seemed to be a problem, and I signed it.

"So, are you ready for your training?" she asked.

"Sure."

My training was under an hour long and primarily consisted of Matangi giving me a more detailed tour of the property, telling me about the native plants, and showing me how to use some of the utilities.

During the tour, something Matangi said reminded me of what Wayne had told me earlier. Before I'd arrived, Matangi and Barb had joked that I was the "male Molly." Apparently, Molly had been a volunteer that asked lots of questions about living in Hawaii before her arrival. She had been concerned about the intensity of the sun, how many mosquitos there were, and other details that are completely reasonable for someone to be concerned about if they've never lived in the tropics before. Since I'd asked similar questions and was also good with computers, they drew a strong comparison between us.

From what Wayne had told me, it sounded like Matangi was anxious about analytical people volunteering at the Community. But didn't she realize that if one wants a computer expert, they must have an analytical side? After all, coding *is* analysis.

That afternoon, I talked to Wayne in a quiet little corner of the property, watching him smoke. Thankfully, he wasn't smoking cigarettes, which ooze probably the most disgusting aroma that humans manufacture.

While I was quite aware of the downsides of smoke, I didn't condemn him for it. In fact, there were occasions when I enjoyed ganja, too, though in limited doses because of my sensitivity. (I still have never used, and have no desire to use, tobacco.)

Wayne and I had talked at this quiet little corner once or twice before, but now that it was just us, I felt comfortable opening up to him more. I intuitively felt that he would understand where I was coming from.

I gave him a quick summary of how Matangi had felt harsh on multiple occasions. Was this how she treated all volunteers? Wayne nodded, saying that she could be pretty excitable, but that was just because of her passion for the Community.

"Mmm, yeah. I just wish I hadn't had that misunderstanding with Barb. I'm worried that it got me off on the wrong foot here. Since then, I feel like Matangi hasn't trusted me, that perhaps she's fixating on that one incident. But Barb and I had a great conversation afterward, and, unless she's being disingenuous, Barb has forgiven me. I'm just concerned that Matangi hasn't."

Wayne furrowed his eyebrows and was silent for a few moments while he composed his thoughts. "Andrew, this place is really different from what you are used to. We're living in community here, and people can be sensitive. But if you want things to go well, you need to *choose* the dominant voices in your head. If you listen to the wrong ones, you'll only hurt yourself. You *choose* who you want to be. So who do you want to be?"

I found his words oddly resonant, and we explored the question. The conversation ebbed and flowed naturally, from the topics of harmony, to travel, and even the concept of past lives. Wayne said that he believed some of the voices in our head are personalities from past lives, but we could always decide which ones we focused on.

Talking to Wayne felt easy, and I was thankful that I'd met two people so far, him and Johann, who I felt were truly on my wavelength. He encouraged me to be patient with Matangi. Apparently, Matangi had told him a bit about her past, and she'd had a challenging childhood, to say the least.

Upon hearing that, something new clicked into place for me. It helped explain some of the anger I'd seen burst out of her.

Wayne and I shared stories for what felt like hours, and through his eyes I grew to understand a few of the other volunteers better. One story in particular stuck out in my mind, about how he once combined tequila and Jägermeister, resulting in a serious memory blackout. I made a mental note never to combine them.

After a while, I found myself itching to go for a walk. The conversation had naturally come to a lull, and I thanked Wayne for being so refreshingly honest with me. I told him I hoped we could have more such talks, and he was confident that we would.

A few days later, I searched the property for a couple of flowers to press into an envelope and send to my mom for Mother's Day. Every year, I try to do something to remind my mother how special she is, and that year I had the opportunity to send her flowers that she'd never even heard of before. I surveyed the property and collected a few of the abundant flowers, and out of the corner of my eye, I saw the unmistakable red streak of a northern cardinal fly through the air.

As I usually do when I see something perplexing, I tilted my head and squinted at it. The bird flitted from one *Monstera* leaf to the other. There was no mistaking what it was. It was definitely a northern cardinal. The question was, how did it get here? Didn't this bird belong on the mainland?

I resumed work on my Mother's Day card, carefully arranging a few of the flowers between some thick construction paper, pressing them flat, and writing a short note on the outside of the pressing. Once it was all sealed up, I realized that it was heavier than most cards. And I only had one stamp, so I taped a few quarters to it, just to be safe.

That night, Matangi wanted everyone to join her and Barb out to dinner to celebrate her impending departure, and we drove down to Ning's Thai Cuisine, which is not only the best Thai food in Puna, but probably my favorite restaurant in the town. It was good to see everyone around one table, and we ate delicious food and were merry.

Everyone paid for themselves, and when we finally left the restaurant, utterly satisfied and happy, we heard live music down the street and followed the sound. Farther down, we found a full band playing a mix of rock and reggae in front of Island Naturals Market, complete with a drum kit, three guitars, and a bass; and we jammed out to the music for a good long while, dancing in the store's parking lot. Everyone was having a blast, and after a while I was shocked to find Johann dancing right behind me!

I was happy to hear that he'd been doing well and was house sitting for a friend. He told me that the performance was part of the Puna Music Festival, which happened every May. When I asked him if he would come to the next Taco Tuesday at Cinderland, he said he'd do his best to make it.

Soon after, the other volunteers said they wanted to take the party back to the Community, and it didn't take long before we had returned to the jungle, various liqueurs and beers littering the table.

Laughter and merriment followed, and it was a good night. Anne-Marie's face flushed from laughing so hard; Larkin was wearing a cute red dress and radiated sweetness; and Wayne's reassuring energy felt like an anchor that the entire group was linked to.

Thankfully, my first official weekend shift was pretty quiet, and Matangi left right in the middle of it. Preparing for a long flight always has some stress associated with it, and the stress of Matangi's trip to the mainland had been building for days.

When she was at last safely on her way, most of us at the Community breathed a sigh of relief. Barb left around this time, too, and the group dynamic felt more relaxed than it had before.

Even from thousands of miles away, Matangi would manage all of the volunteers, including myself, remotely. I had done plenty of remote work before, but this felt like an interesting reversal, and I promised myself that I would work with Matangi professionally and calmly, even if she had another outburst.

Toward the end of my weekend shift, Anne-Marie and Larkin were talking at the community table across from me as I worked. When Larkin asked me if I'd ever paid Stanley for the ride to Green Sand Beach, I winced, sensing what was coming.

"He told me not to worry about it, actually."

Larkin frowned. "So you're not going to give him anything? He took us all the way there, so I gave him some money. You should, too."

"Yeah, Andrew," Anne-Marie said, "And as a long-term volunteer, you're representing the Community. You're better than that."

I cringed. At the time, money was pretty tight for me. As it was, I was buying "reduced" bananas to save cash. (Reduced bananas are bunches that are a bit old and brown, so they're sold for about half the usual price.)

Still, Larkin and Anne-Marie were right. Even though Stanley had never asked about it again or had even hinted anything, I knew that I should give him something. I was being too stingy, and I knew it.

"I'm sorry," I said, feeling suddenly guilty. "He told me not to worry about it, so I forgot about it. But I think you guys are right. Money is tight for me right now, but I'll give him my share of the ride down. And I'll apologize."

"Good," Larkin nodded.

I didn't tell them, but I suddenly felt like utter crap. I had been too stingy, and later on I found Stanley and shared my feelings. He accepted the money with gratitude. Perhaps it was my subjective perspective of having forgiven myself, or perhaps it was just because Matangi had left, but the Community felt more harmonious after that.

And just as this calm settled in, the entire community held a great potluck the following Monday, and Anne-Marie baked the most delicious glazed cinnamon rolls I'd ever tasted in my life.

A new character joined us on the property, too, named Miguel. He was probably the oldest guest that we hosted during my time there, bearing a distinguished face like a medieval king, and he almost always wore collared dress shirts, usually in Hawaiian patterns.

Miguel was visiting the Big Island alone and seemed quite proud of his life. He owned a lovely home and had a beautiful girlfriend back on the mainland, eager to show pictures of both to us. He was instantly friendly and disarming but somewhat guarded, possessing a particular glint of something in his eye. Whether it was mischief or something else, I could never tell.

We never learned why his girlfriend didn't join him on his trip to Hawaii, and after a few days at the Community, Wayne and I came up with the theory that he might have been a Navy SEAL once. Our suspicion grew when he mentioned offhand that he was once in the military, but when one of us asked about it, he would only respond vaguely or evade the question, saying how he felt that chapter of his life was far behind him.

Of course, this only fueled our theory, and with each new vague statement, the more magnificent and legendary his past became in our minds. At the very least, we liked the *idea* of having a former SEAL among us, and it did line up with his disarming, yet guarded, personality.

So when Miguel the Seal joined us at that Great Monday Potluck, Wayne and I paid special attention to anything that might slip out of his mouth.

Alas, he was careful, and few words escaped his smiling lips, except for comments on the music. He liked Daft Punk, and he also loved the guacamole I made. In short, he had good taste.

On the following day, two significant events occurred.

As I was about to hitchhike into town to get more food, I made a passing comment to Anne-Marie about how expensive food was on the island. Staple food items weren't too bad, but a lot of stuff was more expensive than I was used to. She asked me if I'd tried signing up for the Supplemental Nutritional Assistance Program (SNAP), also known as electronic benefit transfer. I had not, and she proceeded to give me a crash course in government food assistance programs.

As I came to discover, almost everyone work-trading in Puna relied on some government assistance to pay for food.

Apparently, it was quite easy to qualify for SNAP if one was work-trading and only getting a place to sleep in exchange for work. (Later, I learned that most people with a net income of less than around $1,000 per month will qualify for something.)

And for the first time I realized that, in the eyes of everyone on the mainland, we were considered poor. What a strange idea, I thought. Paradoxically, even though I wasn't making much money there, I felt more rich and abundant in Puna than anywhere else I'd ever lived. Perhaps it was the abundance of exotic, delicious fruit all around me. Perhaps it was the sense of community that had become part of my daily reality. Or perhaps it was just the sheer beauty of the entire island, but I felt anything but poor. I felt rich.

Even so, all of the volunteers only got a place to stay in exchange for their work, with perhaps a couple of dollars a week in tips, if one was lucky.

Buoyed by Anne-Marie's confidence that I would qualify, I hitchhiked all the way up to Hilo, a nearly hour-long drive. The office was a bit off of the beaten path, and I walked a few extra blocks to get to the building, a long white building complex that was adjacent to a Hawaiian candy shop.

I pulled open one of the glass doors and entered a large room that had been split up with low, cubicle dividers. A series of chairs lined the wall, and a sign told me to take a number. Tension rose within me. What was I doing? I'd never applied for any government programs before. But coming to Hawaii had meant starting over in many ways. All I could be was honest, so I took a number.

To my delight, my waitlist number was 42, one of the luckiest numbers in the universe. I was so surprised by this that I snapped a photo of it, just to have proof of the event later.

As I waited, I read the eligibility form, a mammoth-sized document of about 20 oversized pages. I answered everything honestly, except for my bank account numbers. That question gave me the creeps, not to mention representing a huge security risk. (Later, I learned that this wasn't required information and very few people wrote their account numbers in.)

Soon after, I was guided to a cubicle and met with a worker, which was someone who figured out if I was eligible and had the authority to give me food benefits or not. The worker confirmed with me that I was work-trading and excused herself.

To my surprise, she returned a short time later with a small plastic card with a red flower on it. The worker explained that it worked like a debit card and that my first purchase had to be under $5 to activate it. In five months, I would get an update letter to review if I was still eligible. I would also get a letter in about a week with my pin code. I asked a few clarification questions and was soon on my way, with what felt like a strange new power in my possession.

That night, I headed up to Cinderland for my fourth Taco Tuesday in a row, and on my hitchhike over, I was picked up by a friendly guy who was quick to mention that his car was 100% biodiesel. He even refined the vegetable oils himself, and we exchanged phone numbers. Perhaps I could see how he made the fuel sometime.

He dropped me off at the long gravel road that led into Cinderland, and the evening proceeded as planned. We had a beautiful circle song and fresh, delicious tacos. Except that this time, a bunch of people were getting their faces painted. After enjoying the jungle drums for some time, I wandered back over to the central table in the kitchen area, happy to see Doran. He told me that he was sad to be leaving soon. That's right; he was leaving on May 17, in just three days.

Part of me couldn't believe that I'd been on the Big Island for over three weeks. Time flowed at a strange pace that I still couldn't pin down, but I loved it anyway.

"You know, you're like a little buddha. You've lived out of your small pack this whole time. I think you're the first person who travels with even less stuff than I do. I'm really going to miss you, man."

He smiled. "Thanks. I'm going to miss you, too. But I've got to go; more adventures ahead." He pointed to a shirtless man next to him. "Have you met Noah? I think you'd like him."

I looked over. The shirtless guy wore thin-rimmed glasses and had an air of humility about him.

"Hi, there!" I said, introducing myself.

"Good to meet you!" Noah said in a deep voice. "How long have you been on the island?"

I told him I'd been there for just under a month, and as we talked, I was struck by how he spoke, getting the impression that he was possibly the most well-read person I'd met yet on the island. He spoke with a gentle conviction and articulated his words carefully. Listening to him speak was like hearing a well-written book woven out of elegant, elevated language. He went on and on about how the island was changing him from the inside out. I learned that he was originally from the East Coast, but in his entire life he'd never felt more loved and connected to Humanity than in Puna.

I wasn't surprised. The truth, that we were all sharing and caring for this island together, was something that we all understood, at least most of us who visited Cinderland.

After a while, I checked my iPod. It was nearly 10:00 PM, and I still didn't have a ride back to the Community. I bid Noah farewell and hugged Doran goodbye, telling them I was going to find a ride.

"Safe travels, my friend."

He nodded. "We'll stay in touch. Safe travels!"

It didn't take me long to find someone else heading my direction, and I found my way back to the Community just before midnight.

As a district, Puna was so unique, so quirky and diverse. But to anyone who had come to call Puna their home, they recognized their connection to the land and to each other, and that was beautiful.

Unfortunately, sometimes visitors came with other expectations and failed to recognize the love all around them, as I would soon learn.

CHAPTER 12

WHAT IF I BURN THIS PLACE DOWN?

The next two weeks flew by almost effortlessly, except of course for the day someone threatened to burn the whole place down.

With smiling faces, Wayne and Anne-Marie told me that two of their friends, Ramsey and Esmeralda, were visiting from the mainland. Their main purpose for coming to the island was to have what I can only describe as a dolphin-assisted birth, which I've come to realize is actually a real practice. The couple wanted to swim with the dolphins before, and possibly during, the birth of their child.

Some people are quite passionate about the spiritual connection between dolphins and humans, but since I never saw a dolphin during my adventure, I cannot speak to this connection personally. (I can, however, talk about the human-octopus connection, but we'll get to that later.)

In seeking to catch up with Wayne and Anne-Marie, the couple opted to stay at the Community for the two weeks leading up to the birth, and I was looking forward to meeting the couple that they had spoken of so highly.

As I've mentioned before, it rained just about every single day on the island, if only for a brief period. After all, it was a tropical rainforest, and almost everyone who comes to the Big Island knows to be prepared. But Esmeralda and Ramsey didn't seem to realize this fairly obvious fact.

For context, I have to retell some events that I wasn't personally present for, but here's how Wayne explained it to me.

It all started when Wayne got a call from Ramsey. Apparently, he and Esmeralda had hitchhiked into town to go to the grocery store and found that it was raining once they got back outside. They wanted Wayne to take Matangi's vehicle up to Pahoa town to come and pick them up. The only problem was, Matangi had specifically forbidden any of the volunteers to use the vehicle except for supply runs and to pick up guests from the airport. And as one can imagine, no one wanted to get on Matangi's bad side.

Wayne patiently explained this, but Ramsey's voice only grew louder and louder until he was yelling right into his ear. Wayne hung up. When he turned to me, he wore a pained expression and said nothing, walking past me to go tell Anne-Marie what had happened. She supported Wayne's decision. Their friends could wait for the rain to pass and then hitch back. Then Wayne called Matangi to get her advice, and she maintained that we were not to use the company vehicle for such trips. At any rate, they could take the bus back in an hour or so.

Over an hour later, they showed up at the Community, clothes wet from the rain, and Ramsey was so angry that he didn't even speak to Wayne at first. Both he and Esmeralda went to the restroom to clean up and towel off; and Wayne, Anne-Marie, and I waited in the common area, wondering what we should do. We all felt bad that they walked back in the rain, but the vehicle was not ours; it was Matangi's. We were only allowed to use it under limited circumstances, and after all, there had been other options available to them.

When Ramsey reentered the common area, we all involuntarily tensed up for a moment, expecting his anger.

"I hope you're all proud of what you did today, making a pregnant woman walk for miles in the pouring rain." His sharp glare shifted from me to Wayne and finally Anne-Marie.

"I'm sorry, man," Wayne began, "we had no choice. We're not allowed to rescue guests with Matangi's car. We even called Matangi; she said no."

Ramsey's face twisted in anger. "You made a pregnant woman walk in a downpour!" he yelled. "I thought you guys were our friends!"

"What were we supposed to do?" Wayne winced. "You both seem fine. We feel really bad about it, but it's not our vehicle."

"What if she gets pneumonia now, Wayne?" Ramsey continued. "That will be *your* fault!"

"Bullshit!" Anne-Marie shouted back. "You were the ones who went out without an umbrella. You're our friends, but we're *not* your parents. We did everything we could, and also, we're not responsible for you."

Esmeralda seethed with contempt, narrowing her gaze at Wayne and Anne-Marie, as if she were trying to burn a hole in their skulls using only her mind. Finally, she excused herself, saying something about how she didn't feel that great and was going to lie down.

At seeing her leave, Ramsey started ranting around the common area, railing against Wayne, Anne-Marie, and Matangi. Miraculously, no other volunteers were around for this embarrassing display.

"Dude," Wayne said, walking up to him, "please calm down. It could have been worse. You guys are okay."

Ramsey kept ranting.

"Wayne is right," I said. "Shouting isn't helping anything."

"Like I said man, we feel terrible," Wayne said, "but there was nothing we could do. Please, just calm down."

"Yeah? Well, what if I burn this place down?" he shouted back to Wayne, walking in the other direction. "What if I burn this place to the ground?"

His words changed the energy in the room. Such a violent thought made the common space feel dangerous and unfamiliar. The situation had become overblown, and it needed to stop.

Wayne's so-called friends had gone from being angry to being threatening and toxic.

I stood up from the corner chair and turned to Ramsey. "Hey, they did everything they could. It's not their car, and if you have a complaint, then you're free to contact Matangi. Getting angry doesn't solve anything."

Ramsey walked over to me, puffing out his chest. "You'd better shut up before I bash your face in!"

I instinctively backed away.

"You've gone too far!" Wayne shouted back. "I'm calling the owner. We don't tolerate threats here." He waved for me and Anne-Marie to follow him, and we walked over to the small main office.

Now that it was just us, I had a chance to catch my breath, and I noticed that Anne-Marie's eyes were wet with tears. Wayne called up Matangi and described the situation in detail. Since the phone volume was loud, I could easily hear Matangi's responses to Wayne's questions. I remember her saying, "He has made a threat to the property and to Andrew, which makes this a criminal situation. Wayne, you need to call the police and tell them what has happened."

Wayne nodded, a coldness washing over his face. "Okay."

"It's going to be okay," Matangi reassured him. "Just handle this calmly and professionally. Is Anne-Marie there?"

"Yeah." Wayne handed her the phone.

"Anne-Marie, are you okay?"

"Yeah," she whispered, "I just can't believe they're acting this way. I thought they were our friends, and now…" She sniffed, wiping some tears from her eyes. "I'm embarrassed, and I'm very hurt by their behavior."

"It'll be okay, Anne-Marie," Matangi said. "Call me after you notify the police. Tell the police that the owner wants both of them to leave the premises as soon as possible. I can talk to them if necessary."

"Okay," she said, "talk to you soon."

I cannot recall who called the police, but when they arrived a short time later, Wayne walked up to me, tension filling his face.

"Hey dude, the cops are here. Can you do me a favor? Can you deal with them? Cops make me nervous. Do you mind?"

I nodded. "I don't mind at all. No worries."

I met the officers at the entrance and let them in, retelling the story in the most concise way I could.

They asked me where the disturber of the peace was, and when I turned around, I noticed that Esmeralda was talking to Ramsey over by the main building. I pointed over to them and saw Ramsey shake his head, a dark expression passing over his face. I asked the officers if they needed anything else. They said no, so I told them that I would be up by the entrance.

A moment later, I ran into Wayne.

"How's it going?" he asked, his eyes glancing up to where the cops were.

"Well, the police are talking with them. I gotta say, I'm not sure how they're going to react."

"They threatened the property and you personally. I'm so sorry, Andrew. They've never been like this before."

I stared into his dark eyes. "You did what you had to do. We live here; we're subject to this place's rules. You didn't do anything wrong, Wayne. Remember that."

Farther up, the police turned around and began walking back over to us.

"Okay, man. Just let me know how it went." Wayne walked back to the office, making himself scarce.

Once again, it was just me and the police. They explained that the couple were happy to leave, but that the agreement they signed gave them 48 hours to find another place to stay. I thanked the police for their help and went to find Wayne who called Matangi. We confirmed that they had two days to find somewhere else to go, and soon the couple had disappeared into their sleeping quarters, leaving the property in an eerie silence.

"I'm sorry that this had to happen," Wayne said.

"It's okay," I said. "It's not your fault. Ramsey just lost it."

Wayne shook his head, saying something about how they were different from how he and Anne-Marie remembered them.

Needless to say, the next couple days were awkward, and everyone avoided making eye contact with them in the common areas. In the end, it took them three days to find another place. After the second day, they assured us they'd found a place and were moving the following day, so no one made a big deal about it. We just wanted them to leave peacefully.

On the positive side, the whole ordeal had brought the three of us much closer together, strengthening an alliance that would prove pivotal later on.

I have no idea if Esmeralda ever gave birth to their child in the ocean or not, and as far as I know, Wayne and Anne-Marie never saw them again after that.

CHAPTER 13

THE MAGIC OF THE RED ROAD

On the southeast edge of the Big Island, there is a lovely route, officially called Kapoho Kalapana Road, that hugs the rugged coastline of the island. Today, it's paved with smooth asphalt, but for most of its history it was paved with red cinder gravel, which is where it gets its local name: The Red Road.

Only a tiny portion at the end of the road still has any red cinder, but that's the only name I ever heard anyone call it when I was there.

In short, the Red Road is a magnificent drive. Barely wide enough to contain two lanes at points, the route leads past rocky coastlines, impenetrable rainforest, black sand beaches, oceanside parks, and tucked-away neighborhoods. The road comes so close to the edge of the island that one can often see waves crashing just ahead, and at points the trees are so thick that the road cuts a tunnel through the forest itself.

Even though I cruised down that road dozens upon dozens of times during my adventure, I never tired of it, especially when rainbows regularly formed high above me, or when the sun painted the sky in bright oranges and reds, as it so often did to signal the end of another Hawaiian day.

On one such day, I headed down to Isaac Hale Beach Park, which was a good place to swim and also happened to have the only boat landing in all of Puna.

Plus, I needed something to distract me from one of my ears, which had become partially plugged a few days before. Losing most of my hearing in one ear was disorienting to say the least, and I came to realize much later that it was probably caused by airborne mold or other fungi near where I was sleeping.

For a long time, I thought Isaac Hale Beach Park was pronounced Isaac "Ha-lay" after the Hawaiian word for house, but after further research I learned that the park was named in honor of Private Isaac K. Hale who fought in the Korean War. In recognizing this, I will mention that the correct pronunciation of the veteran's name is "hail" just like the weather phenomenon.

That day, about a dozen people, mostly kids, were swimming near the boat landing, a gentle incline nestled within an inlet, shielded from the waves. Since I hadn't swum in the ocean in many years, I joined the kids who were swimming in a calmer spot, removing my shoes and carefully placing my daypack in view, beside a kind family who agreed to watch it for me.

Carefully, I slipped in. I had no life jacket or swimming flippers, but there was a lifeguard on duty, so I didn't worry. After getting more comfortable with the water, I practiced the back stroke and found that I remembered my childhood swimming lessons well enough.

Even so, some waves disturbed the inlet, and I had a panicked moment when I accidentally swallowed some salt water. I forced myself to stay calm as I caught my breath, trying not to flail as I swam over to the edge of the boat landing. The salt water burned inside my nose, and I struggled to clear my sinuses as I held onto one of the boulders near a concrete wall.

I pulled myself up out of the water, wishing that I had swimming flippers, and dried off, catching my breath and slipping my shoes on. It had been years since I'd felt the burn of saltwater in my nose, and the feeling had brought me back to a memory of when I was very young and a wave had washed over me as I played in the sand back in California. I'd never forget that. And didn't one of my characters get hit with a wall of water in the sequel that I was in the middle of writing? I would have to remember to describe the feeling of how saltwater burns.

To my surprise, I ran into Johann a few minutes later. He was taking the afternoon to explore and relax just as I was, and we ended up walking over to the intersection to hitchhike west down the Red Road, toward Kalapana.

The intersection above Isaac Hale park usually had decent traffic, but on that particular day, traffic was sparse. The few who passed by weren't inclined to pick us up, and as we waited, I noticed some vines hanging down from the trees nearby.

"Hey, do you think that vine could support a person's weight?" I wondered.

"Let's see!" He reached out and grabbed the woody vine, about as wide as a quarter, and swung out over the bushes before swinging back over to the road and finally letting go.

Soon, I was swinging in wide arcs over the grass, my shorts still dripping with salt water from my swim earlier. It was a blast, and I asked if he could snap a picture of me swinging on the vine. We ended up taking a series of silly photos of both of us swinging around like jungle men, and later we had a good laugh looking at our goofy expressions in the photos.

In the end, we decided to walk instead of hitchhike. We needed to dry off more anyway, so we followed the Red Road west as it cut through an especially thick patch of rainforest. After about a half hour, we came upon a gap in the forest where two wooden stools had been placed on the grass near the edge of a rocky cliff. At this welcome patch of open grass, we took a break, and I took that chance to photograph the majestic cliff faces, the colors of the rock changing with each layer until the rocks were light brown where the waves crashed against them.

As we rested, I asked Johann how the house sitting had been going, and he was sad to admit that the house had been broken into while he'd been out. The doors had been locked, but someone had broken in anyway, stealing his laptop and some other things. He was understandably concerned about the owner's reaction to learning about the incident, and I tried to comfort him as best I could. Later, I learned that the particular neighborhood that the house was in was especially susceptible to burglary, and it hadn't been the first time the house had been broken into.

"I'm sorry, Johann." I said. "That sucks. But maybe they'll find out who did it. There's still a chance they'll recover the stuff."

"Maybe."

"Hey, it's getting late. You wanna hitchhike down to Kalapana and get a sandwich?" I smiled. "It'll make you feel better; the café there makes delicious vegetarian sandwiches."

He smiled back. "Okay."

Eventually, we arrived at the end of the Red Road, where the asphalt ended and became red cinder once more. It was just around dinner time when we arrived at the café, and they made us two delicious sandwiches with fresh salads on the side, topped with little purple flowers. It all looked so good that I couldn't help but snap a photo to preserve the memory, my final photo in the month of May.

CHAPTER 14

NEVER ENOUGH

For the first few weeks, I felt that Matangi and I were working together pretty well. Even though she had occasional bursts of frustration or anger, I remembered what Wayne had told me about her challenging past. And I tried not to worry about some of the stories I'd heard from other people around Puna, stories of how they'd come to Matangi's community and quickly grew weary of the environment there.

After all, maybe they were just a bad match for the place. I still really enjoyed working with Wayne and Anne-Marie, but as the weeks passed, I grew more and more concerned about my relationship with Matangi.

Without revealing any identifiable aspects of the Community, I'll mention that I had very limited options of places to do computer work and still have access to electricity and internet signal. The best place was in a common area where insects and mosquitos would frequently find me working, so I tried insect repellent; but apparently my blood was an incredible lure to the insects nearby since it didn't work that well.

I eventually resorted to a special candle to repel them. It was mostly effective, but created smoke that was an additional challenge for me since I am sensitive to smoke. I felt like the Community environment itself was starting to work against me.

Website development, graphic design, and most of the other computer work that I did requires a lot of focus to do well, and I wanted to complete every project that Matangi assigned to me with a high level of quality. If I did any less, I'd feel that I wasn't reflecting my values in my work; and the fact that, at the time of this book's publication, Matangi's website still uses much of the code and design elements that I built speaks to the quality of the work that I did for her.

Even so, most of the time our phone conversations ended with me feeling disappointed in myself. But I tried to be patient and not let our differences get in the way of our relationship.

Frankly, it's challenging to describe the full reality of that situation. I enjoyed being the website administrator and lead graphic designer. I even enjoyed cleaning the common areas, processing volunteer payments, and taking all business-related calls, but I found it difficult to do all of these tasks in addition to completing her web projects on the timetable that she wanted. And I found the frequent interruptions the most challenging part of the position.

I'm not sure if Matangi simply didn't get along with analytical people in the first place, as Wayne had hinted at weeks earlier, but she didn't seem to understand that, when I was interrupted in the middle of writing website code, it would necessarily take me time to get back into a flow-state of doing focused, quality work.

The stakes felt high, too. After all, no other volunteer could accidentally break the entire website, Matangi's main source of new volunteers, if they weren't paying close attention. To this day, I'm not sure if Matangi didn't comprehend the inefficient workflow she forced upon me or didn't really care, but she definitely didn't act like interrupting me in the middle of editing the website database was a problem. As I mentioned, that type of work takes a lot of focus to do well, and I struggled to find balance within it all.

Originally, we wanted to create a special technical position for me, but I ended up feeling pushed into taking the standard weekend shift, plus a cornucopia of website, database, and design work on top of that. In the end, it was an odd, hybrid-position, and after a while, I felt that more expectations were placed on me than any other volunteer at the Community. This alone could have been a point of pride, but the consistent negativity from Matangi wore down my energy.

To be clear, I wasn't the only person working hard. She always pushed her volunteers to do more during their work shifts, even when they were being productive. But no one was expected to perform with the range and attention to detail that my hybrid position required.

Weeks before, I had hoped that distance might help my relationship with Matangi, that communicating via email would encourage both of us to communicate more clearly, but the distance only seemed to exacerbate any miscommunication. After a while, I realized that her emails primarily contained negative comments about what she wished I had completed on a given day instead of recognition of what I had actually finished.

Even worse, she resented the fact that I wasn't doing more physical labor, even though we had agreed that I was there to focus on the technical side, as part of my hybrid position.

When I realized her resentment, I should have known that there would be troubles ahead and started looking for another place immediately, one that was a better fit for me, but I didn't hunt one down like I should have. Sure, I looked around for a better place, but I could have looked more intently, with more determination. Perhaps I would have saved myself a lot of the pain that was to come.

As time went on, my heart sunk lower and lower as I realized that, no matter how hard I tried, it felt like my work was never enough for Matangi.

Take the following story, for example.

One day, Matangi sent me a short email saying that she wanted some good photos showing off the plants and property, and I felt excited about this new project. After spending the morning cleaning, I went out to capture some of the beauty of the flora and fauna of the land. Out of the dozens of photos I took, I ended up with a collection of 12 plant photos that beautifully captured the exotic plant life of the area. I cropped and optimized them for the website, sending them to Matangi before I got back to some other website work she'd assigned.

The following morning, she berated me for using an entire shift to take photos, saying that they were just artistic shots of plants—except that I *hadn't* taken an entire shift to do that. I had cleaned and made progress on other web projects, as well. But apparently, she wanted photos of some of the new developments on the property, even though she'd never specified that. Then she lectured me about what it meant to be a leader. I wanted to tell her that her email asking for photos had been too vague, but I held back. I didn't feel that such a response would help her calm down or even be professional.

Matangi's response shocked and discouraged me. I had gotten a lot done besides taking photos that day, but she either didn't realize or didn't care.

I tried to give her the benefit of the doubt and wrote her an email, describing to her more precisely how I was spending my time. I also vowed to explain myself in greater detail.

In her email response, she took that opportunity to tell me that she thought I was a slow cleaner, despite the fact that she'd seen me clean only once or twice before she left the island. She said that I shouldn't use cleaning work as an excuse to do less computer work.

I considered telling her how it was challenging that the best work space was open to the air, where bugs could slow me down, but I didn't. The common area was one of the few spaces that had electricity, internet signal, and a flat surface to work on; and if I told her it wasn't good enough, it would only sound like complaining to her.

I read her email again and shook my head in bewilderment, getting the feeling that even if I worked for 48 hours straight, she still wouldn't be satisfied.

Over the next several weeks, I made efforts to communicate more clearly, and this helped, for a while at least. When I sent her a photo of the property at sunset, she berated me for messing with the color too much.

I hadn't changed the color at all. And when I told her that the photo reflected the true color of the sunset on the clouds that evening, she apologized.

Even so, I fell in love with Puna throughout this time, spending less and less time at the Community. I still loved hanging out with Wayne and Anne-Marie, but my work life was rapidly becoming toxic. And no matter what I did, it didn't seem to improve. I had to find another opportunity, another place to call home on the island.

Of course, I could have tried to get a traditional job, but work was pretty scarce in Puna, and I wanted to retain as much of my time-flexibility as possible. At that time in my life, having five days a week completely free on the Big Island felt like a beautiful luxury. It gave me time to write, too.

My first novel, *The Truth Beyond the Sky*, had a good spike in sales in May, and I wanted to start writing the sequel while the iron was hot. If I changed my situation, I might not find another agreement that afforded me so much time to write, either. My outline for the book was finally coming together, and I would start the rough draft soon.

Many thoughts were swirling around my head in June, and in the end, I decided to make the best of it, hoping that I would earn Matangi's trust over time. I told myself that as long as I was doing quality work, things should improve; so instead of focusing on my demotivating work situation, I focused on exploring the island, sending out a few Couchsurfing.com requests to some hosts in Hilo.

If I was going to fully explore and appreciate the largest settlement on the Big Island, I needed to stay there overnight. And, seemingly in correlation with this new resolution, my ear cleared up completely.

CHAPTER 15

HILO & NEARBY WATERFALLS

I felt so happy that my hearing was back to normal. It was as if my whole head could breathe again, and I did more research on Hilo, deciding what I wanted to see when I was there. All the while, thoughts of the upcoming solstice were rolling around in the back of my mind. On the solstice, I would start writing the sequel to my first book. But until then, it was time to finally get out of Pahoa and explore Hilo itself.

And so, one Thursday morning, I hitchhiked over to the four-way intersection just south of Pahoa, beginning a two week stint of Hilo adventures. Thankfully, it didn't take long before someone responded to my outstretched thumb, pulling safely over to the shoulder.

Less than an hour later, I was dropped off in the heart of Hilo, brimming with excitement over my impending explorations. I wandered around the bay front, lined with various shops, cafés, and museums that had a remarkably clear view of the Hilo Bay ahead. And once again, I wondered why the land bordering the bay was left mostly unused, merely covered in green grass. The bus depot and a large gazebo were the only noticeable buildings to the north of Mamalahoa Highway as it skirted the edge of the city.

I popped into a grocery store called Abundant Life and grabbed a veggie wrap before resuming my walk around town. And as I headed east along the strip, I looked out onto the bay to my left. Something about the green space intrigued me.

Why was it so clear of buildings? It was beachfront property, after all. Didn't developers like to use up such space as quickly as possible, usually ruining the view? It wouldn't be until I reached Coconut Island that I would finally learn the answer.

Heading east, I passed towering banyan trees that were at least three times larger than any maple I'd ever seen before. I walked by Bay Front park, crossed a bridge, and headed toward Liliuokalani Gardens, a beautifully maintained landmark that reminded me of an arboretum. But I didn't go inside. Something else caught my eye: a narrow footbridge ahead that spanned part of the bay, leading to a tiny island.

Dotted with tall palms, the tiny island called out to me, and I crossed the narrow metal bridge to the other side, finding a wide grassy lawn in the center of the island just ahead, where dozens of people were practicing yoga together. A sidewalk led around the edge of the island, and I followed it to the right, passing a small bay and a stone tower at the far end. It appeared to be the ruins of an old building. Steps led up to the top, and people were using it as a diving platform. And way out in the distance, a faint rainbow stretched up out of the horizon and into the clouds.

Eventually, I reached the other end of the tiny island, where there was a covered area for picnicking; and I pulled out my lunch, savoring the colorful veggie wrap as the waves crashed against the dark boulders ahead. As I ate, a team of six rowed across the bay in a long white craft. And beyond, I could easily see the far northern side of the bay, white mist suspended over the trees as if they were part of a dream.

Once I'd finished eating, I followed the sidewalk to the west side of the island, where a few weathered plaques stood under some palms. One plaque explained that the open green area in the center of Coconut Island, along with most of the Hilo bay front, had been devastated by a tsunami in April 1946, and then again in May 1960.

Afterward, it became clear to the residents that tsunamis would continue to hit Hilo from time to time, and since the redevelopment of the old bay front was seen as ultimately futile, they designated the entire area as recreational land. That's why Hilo was given the nickname "City of Parks."

I studied a black and white photo beside the text, depicting the nearby land inundated with water. Hopefully, I wouldn't be so unlucky as to witness such a disaster.

But what about the seaside hotel to the east? The plaque explained that the hotels behind me had been designed with tsunami resilience in mind and contained reinforced concrete pillars starting on the ground floor. They also had thin walls, allowing any tsunami waves to pass through the ground floor of the hotels with little resistance.

Unsurprisingly, the narrow footbridge to Coconut Island had been destroyed after nearly every tsunami. Only time would tell how long the current bridge would last.

I looked up. The sun was getting low and the clouds were rolling in. I'd since realized how quickly the sun set on Hawaii and headed back over the footbridge. My Couchsurfing host Rob would be home soon, and perhaps we could make some dinner together. As I walked back, I couldn't help but be struck by the beauty of the clouds all around me, splashed in the reds and magentas of the Hawaiian sunset.

Rob proved to be a generous and gracious host. Even better, he wanted help with his Mac mini. I love helping out anyone who hosts me, and he was easy to talk to. He mentioned that he'd been a whistleblower in the Vietnam War, but he didn't seem to have much to say about it, other than his feeling that it was hell on Earth. We got along well, and I was glad I could help him out with his computer. It was a good exchange, and he said he would be happy to have me back again sometime.

Around this time, my dreams also grew more vivid, and my journal entries took on a new flavor.

2013-06-16, Sunday

Last night I had a dream that I was back in Wisconsin, my old-old life...I was standing in the driveway wondering why I ever came back. When I thought of how I was in the wrong place again, I felt a sinking feeling in my stomach. I had made a mistake. I should have stayed in Hawaii longer. Then I woke up and was relieved to still be here. I still had a chance to do what I needed to do. Zahn still hadn't been found by Asha, and the waterfalls still hadn't been photographed.

Reading between the lines, this entry reminds me of how I was excited to resolve the challenges that my characters had got themselves into in the first part of my new book. But to keep things fresh, I had to keep exploring.

On that first exploration of the city, I also visited Rainbow Falls, so named because on sunny mornings around 10:00 AM, rainbows tend to form in the mist around them. I didn't see a rainbow that day, but the falls were nonetheless a sight to behold. Cascading down off a plateau of lava rock about 24 meters above a large pool, the falls were framed beautifully by towering Moluccan albizia trees and verdant ferns, and below, layers of green moss found refuge in the mist that collected on the walls of lava rock on either side. Later, I would come to dislike the albizia trees, which are native to New Guinea, among other places, but in that moment, they struck me as beautiful.

The falls are actually within Hilo city limits, and since they were just about level with the viewing area, it looked possible that I could reach the top of the falls without too much trouble. In fact, I could have sworn I saw a few people already up there.

I made my way down a path that cut through dense rainforest, surprised to find that it had a railing, a rarity for paths on the island. A few minutes later, I came upon a rocky area, punctuated by shallow pools. Carefully stepping around these pools, I eventually reached a boulder just above the falls themselves, perching myself on a comfortable spot where I pulled out a raw fruit cookie that I'd bought earlier. The roar of the waterfall felt soothing, and I could easily see where the Wailuku River flowed east, making its way through a narrow channel toward the sea.

And in that moment, I felt content and happy.

The following week, I hitchhiked up to Hilo once more. Rob wanted to learn about his options for a website, and I was happy to answer his questions. While there, I visited the Pana'ewa Rainforest Zoo, which, according to its website, is the only natural tropical rainforest zoo in the USA.

It also happens to have free admission, and I found it easy to spend hours there, enjoying the stunning red and green eclectus parrots, playful lemurs, camera-shy anteaters, an ancient tortoise that seemed to resent my very existence, a peacock that the zoo felt would be happiest if it just roamed around the zoo freely, and a rare white Bengal tiger that humbled me with its beauty and grace.

But without a doubt, the most impressive spot I visited that month was 'Akaka Falls. And because it was off of the beaten path, Rob offered to take me, saying that we could explore it together, and I gratefully accepted his offer.

About 24 kilometers and 30 minutes later, we arrived at a parking lot beside a large sign where a single park employee stood. We paid the dollar fee per person and walked in, following the looping path past thick undergrowth and banyan trees whose roots spidered over the rocks like otherworldly creatures. The forest canopy was thick above us, and I was grateful that the parks department had gone to such care to provide a path with actual stairs and railings. With so many ravines around, exploring the park without pathways could have been hazardous.

We followed the path to the eastern edge of the loop to the lookout over Kahuna Falls. It fell over 90 meters, but from our angle, we could only see its edge. I could make out patches of white water racing down, but the thick forest made it difficult to get a clear view.

Heading back west, the path led us beside the Kolekole stream far below. Soon, the stream was completely obscured by the thick forest, but once we passed through a patch of banyan trees, the forest grew thinner.

I noticed that a tree trunk ahead had some hearts and letters carved into it. Apparently "A+D" really wanted to let their love be known; I only wish they hadn't injured a tree in the process.

A couple minutes later, I at last saw the white streak of a narrow waterfall in the distance ahead. When we reached the observation point, I was stunned at the sheer immensity of the falls. A sign nearby explained that 'Akaka was a free-falling waterfall, plunging down over 130 meters as one continuous flow, and I looked up once more, watching how the water plummeted over the bare rock, almost straight down into a dark pool that was so far below us that it was difficult to get a clear view. Green and brown moss clung to life on the edge of the cliff face, growing thicker closer to the bottom, and I marveled at this exceptional place, the distant roar of the falls mixing with my thoughts of gratitude.

Another sign nearby mentioned the native goby fish in Kolekole Stream, of which 'Akaka Falls was the most dramatic part. I learned that, after maturing downstream, the o'opu goby must make its way back up the sheer cliff, using its pectoral fins and a suction disc above its belly to scale the 130 meter tall waterfall. Somehow, this 12 centimeter creature reaches the top to lay its eggs in the waters above the falls. Even more astounding, it's not the only species to do this. A native shrimp species performs the same feat!

For comparison, I am about 1.76 meters tall, so to climb up something with the equivalent height ratio, I would have to climb up a sheer cliff over 1,900 meters high. Wow!

After a few more photos, Rob and I headed back to his place to eat and relax. Reading about the goby's life made me tired just thinking about it, and I was happy to be human.

CHAPTER 16

ALIEN FRUIT

The following day was a Friday, but more importantly it was the summer solstice, the day I'd promised myself that I'd start working on my second book, a sequel to my first Mythic Sci-Fi novel, *The Truth Beyond the Sky*. And I began that day by writing the following paragraph in my intention journal:

Today is an auspicious day. Today, on this first day of summer, I begin writing the sequel to my first story. This sequel will affect and move people even more profoundly than the first, and it will be an improvement on the first in every way.

To say that I felt pressure to outdo my first book was an understatement. *The Truth Beyond the Sky* had gotten dozens of glowing, multi-paragraph reviews, and it had only been out for about six months at that point. I'd even received Twitter messages from people that I'd never even met, asking me when the sequel was coming out. So once I'd settled in at the Community, I took time to flesh out an outline, trying to give my characters a fresh call to adventure, even as I was in the midst of my own, rather different, journey.

After many weeks of contemplating, I realized that three ideas resonated with me the most. First, the main character would be female. Second, this book would be about love and connection. And third, I had to raise the stakes this time around. If I wanted to write a trilogy, this second installment would need to provide conflicts to resolve for the third book.

That's all I knew for sure when I sat down in one of the few secluded spots in the Community. As I began, I felt a familiar tension that I always got when I began a big project. What if I couldn't finish this book? What if the first one had been a fluke? Or worse, what if I didn't have the self-discipline to focus on writing in the midst of this paradisical place? What if the underlying stress of being managed by Matangi somehow sabotaged the entire project? Could I find balance?

Perhaps I could find a better work-trade opportunity. There had to be a place that was a better match for me, at least one that wasn't run by a person who felt like a bully most of the time.

I refocused my thoughts, opened my outline, and created a new TextEdit document beside it. Many writers use more complex programs, but when I'm writing, I want everything out of the way. All I want is to see what I've written in crisp text, in Caslon Pro typeface if at all possible. (Caslon Pro is used in the paperback edition of this book. It's close to my heart.)

For a few moments, I reread what I'd written in my outline over the past few weeks. I had a wealth of ideas, but I didn't yet have a clear ending in mind. Still, I had a strong idea for a first chapter, so I decided to dive in. After all, the summer solstice was a strong time to begin, and if everything went to plan, I would have a first draft finished by the winter solstice.

As I stared at the blank document, my heart filled with a mixture of excitement and intimidation at resuming my characters' lives, characters that people all around the world had said that they loved.

An idea hit me, a pattern that would weave through the entire series, and I wrote the first sentence. Even though I would go on to rewrite part of that first chapter, the first line would never change:

Asha felt a chill sweep through her body.

Starting the following Monday, I took a break from Hilo. After all, I'd spent the last two weeks focused on that city. Instead, I explored some corners of Pahoa that I hadn't seen before. In the process, I stumbled upon a small orange goldfish in a pizzeria off of Main Street. The owner said that the fish's name was Bugs, no doubt because of how far his eyes bugged out of his head, jiggling disconcertingly with each twitch of his fins. The owner said that Bugs was the mascot of Pahoa, and I came to learn that almost everyone had met the little goldfish.

A short walk later, I discovered a small fruit stand with wooden shelves stacked with all kinds of exotic foods. While I'd seen some fantastic farmer's markets up to that point, this stand was different. It was open most of the week and had the most impressive little collection of local honey, jams, and fruits that I'd ever seen, all carefully arranged in a cozy kind of way. The trays on the shelves were labeled with names like blue ginger, Philippine purple yams, pink grapefruit, apple bananas, and mamey sapote.

The woman at the counter, Dez, was inviting and happy to teach me about this alien-looking fruit. Originally from Texas, she'd come to the Big Island five years ago and hadn't looked back. She ran the stand with her boyfriend, and when I asked if they were running the stand full-time, she said that they were still working at a homestead to make ends meet. But their goal was to be doing it full-time soon.

Their stand, which primarily featured fruit from local farmers, was a multiyear project, and they were working really hard to grow the business. I found their situation easy to relate to. I wanted to write full-time, but I still hadn't reached that point.

To my surprise, her boyfriend popped his head out from behind the counter, and I gasped to realize that he'd been there the entire time, working on something out of view. He had a quiet, calming presence, and I liked him instantly.

I contemplated getting a small $8 jar of local honey or a mamey sapote, a large fruit with brown leathery skin that Dez had told me contained sweet orange flesh, but in the end I decided on a bunch of apple bananas, a variety of banana that is smaller and sweeter than the Cavendish bananas that are ubiquitous on the mainland.

Something about Dez seemed familiar, and as I walked away, I had the feeling that I would be seeing her and her boyfriend again. Few people had put me so quickly at ease, and I sensed that they genuinely cared about each and every person that they sold food to.

I walked back down to the intersection at the south end of town and stuck out my thumb, and it only took a few short minutes before a kind soul pulled over to the side of the road.

This time, I was picked up by a friendly young woman named Sandi. She asked me where I lived and what I was doing on the island. I told her a bit about the Community and asked her where she was staying. Excitedly, she told me about a meditation center nearby. She loved it there, and in a few weeks they were hosting a 10-day silent meditation retreat. They were also looking for volunteers.

I cleared my throat, considering her invitation. I'd meditated in group settings before and had enjoyed it. I was also actively searching for a change of pace, but the idea of 10 days without speaking gave me pause. I told her I'd have to think about it and asked her the address of the center.

As she dropped me off near the Community, Sandi stressed how much she benefited from the experience and urged me to think about it. I smiled back, saying that I would and thanked her for the ride. As I walked away, I considered her story and made a mental note to hitchhike down to the meditation center that she said was so close.

But how could that be? Out of the dozens of drivers who had picked me up, not to mention everyone else in Puna that I'd talked to, no one I'd met up to that point had ever mentioned a meditation center. Was it just starting up? Clearly, I would have to investigate.

CHAPTER 17

REFLECTIONS & FIREWORKS

On Wednesday, I realized that I'd been missing a major piece of the full experience of living in Puna. Friends had been telling me about Uncle Robert's Wednesday night market for weeks, and now that I had taken a short break from exploring Hilo, that Wednesday was the perfect opportunity to hitch down to the end of the Red Road once more.

Who was Uncle Robert? Why did he have a market? These questions were swirling around my mind as my ride pulled into Uncle Robert's parking lot, a gravel area that bordered the vast Kalapana lava field that stretched on to the west and north.

Even before I stepped out of the car, I heard music in the distance. But something else drew my attention: the sunset. It was descending in smooth orange tones over the black lava field, obscured by thick purple clouds. The scene was otherworldly, and I took a moment to snap a photo before heading down to the main entrance.

From here, I noticed the café that Johann and I had eaten at earlier that month and followed the last stretch of paved road up to the right, where a bunch of people were gathered under a large structure to my left, supported by huge wooden beams. All of it was open to the air, of course, and I walked inside, a flood of information rushing into me at once.

Ahead to the right was a smoothie stand, and beyond it rows of narrow tables were filled with every kind of local product imaginable. To my left, there were wooden picnic tables where some people were eating, and Uncle Robert's sons played traditional Hawaiian music on guitars and ukuleles on a stage in the distance, yellow leis of flowers around their necks. They were quite good, and the dance floor in front of the stage was filled with a dozen or so smiling dancers, mostly couples but there were a few single dancers, too.

The entire place felt so welcoming, and I wandered past tables of delicious homemade breads, jewelry, paintings, and locally-brewed kombucha, the fizzy, fermented drink that I'd first learned about at Cinderland.

I ran into Heartsong again, the musician I'd met at Kehena beach. He didn't have a harmonica this time, but his interactions with the local sellers confirmed my intuitive feeling: everybody knew him, and he seemed happy to see me.

After I'd explored the booths, I sat down at one of the picnic tables and just enjoyed the music, letting the Hawaiian melodies soothe and relax my entire being. I closed my eyes and inhaled slowly, realizing how much I loved it here. Everything felt more harmonious, more joyful, and I was so grateful for that.

I took some time to photograph Uncle Robert's many sons playing on stage, doing my best to capture the celebration of that night. Later, I would learn that, by blood, they were some of the most Hawaiian people I would meet on the island.

Minutes stretched into hours, and as people started leaving, I realized that if I was going to hitchhike back to the Community, I should probably start trying before the crowd thinned out any more. And on my way out, I saw a familiar face in the crowd.

Of course! It was Ganymede, the one who had spearheaded our exploration of Halemaʻumaʻu, the huge lava caldera in the middle of Volcanoes National Park. He greeted me with a smile, and we spent a few minutes catching up. I thanked him once again for facilitating the trip, and he was glad that I had fun. He was on the rainy side of the island for a little while because he was visiting a friend in Hilo.

In the end, we exchanged business cards, and I shook my head in amazement as I detached from the crowd, still reveling in the music. I was starting to feel that, on the island, just about anyone could show up at *any* time.

The following weekend was busier than usual. Matangi had new instructions about what to photograph. Thankfully, she was specific that time, allowing me to deliver something that she was happy with. Matangi was certainly making the most of my camera and photography skills. And I don't blame her.

Most people at the Community only had their phone to take pictures with, and in 2013 the cameras built into cell phones really didn't hold a candle to my Fujifilm camera and its large telephoto lens.

Even so, there was still an undercurrent of friction between me and Matangi that I felt disheartened by, and once again the conflict arose within me. Should I move soon and potentially upset my writing process for my book? Or should I stay where I was and wait until a clearly superior opportunity presented itself?

These thoughts were floating around in my mind when I hitchhiked back up to Hilo the following week for Independence Day. I'd heard that Hilo hosted an excellent fireworks display, and considering it had been two weeks since I'd seen Rob, I called him up and asked him if I could crash on his couch the night of the third.

"Sure!" he said. As long as I didn't mind sharing a space with a couple other couch surfers, I was welcome.

"Thanks again, Rob. I really appreciate it!"

"You're welcome. You remember how to get here, right?"

"Yep," I said. "You're not far from downtown, so it'll be no trouble at all."

Independence Day in Hilo was bound to be a blast. When my ride dropped me off at the bay front on July 3, I noticed a stage set up near the road, and once I reached it, I was surprised by what I saw: dozens of gleaming, classic automobiles.

There were so many cars that they filled up most of the parking lot, and I snapped some shots of Corvette convertibles and classic Mustangs ranging from candy apple red to deep purple, all polished carefully so that they gleamed in the warm tropical sunlight. I'll be the first to admit that I'm not a car guy, but the beauty of these restored vehicles was inspiring.

Later that day, I found a good spot by the bay front where people had collected into small groups. Most of them had brought a folding chair or blanket, and I wished that I'd had the foresight to do the same. Still, with the change of clothes and my laptop, my small daypack was already mostly full.

Since Rob said he wasn't heading down to watch the fireworks and would light off his own later, I wandered around alone, seeing if I recognized anyone I knew. To my delight, I ran into a few people from Cinderland, mostly hippy types with handmade clothing. Although I'd only talked to most of them briefly at Taco Tuesday, they greeted me warmly, as if they knew me well, and offered me a place to sit with them on the blanket they'd brought.

We talked as the day faded, until the sky at last exploded in red and white light. Launched from a ship in the middle of the bay, the fireworks display was pretty good considering that the city had a population of less than 50,000 people. Although the show lasted under 15 minutes, it had good variety, and we all cheered at each exploding firework shell as they rained twinkling colors down over the bay. And the finale was excellent; probably a 12-inch shell! At that size, the colorful explosion filled most of my vision in a dazzling display.

Later that evening, I returned to Rob's place, and we lit a series of small fountains that spewed orange flares from little tubes. All of the fireworks were rather small, probably because of Hilo city laws. Even so, we spent about an hour lighting them off. He just seemed happy to have someone to share them with, and I thanked him again for opening up his home to Couchsurfing members.

The following day, I caught a bus from downtown Hilo back to Pahoa. I'd discovered that it was tricky to hitchhike out of Hilo because one basically had to walk to the edge of the city, and it was pretty far before there was a good place for people to pull over.

As I rode the bus back down, I realized that I dreaded the work shift I had at the Community the following day. I felt resistance to dealing with Matangi's reoccurring negativity.

The clouds outside were splashed with a mix of vanilla and purple light from the evening sun, and I tried to focus on them instead, taking a few long-exposure photos with my camera.

The feelings rose up within me again. There was no denying it: I was dreading going back.

A few minutes later, an older woman with deep lines on her face sat down across from me. She seemed interesting, so I struck up a conversation with her, asking her how she was doing.

She was engaging, and it didn't take long before I opened up to her and told her a bit about what I was struggling with, refraining from naming Matangi, of course. I told her that I felt like no matter what I did, I couldn't earn my boss's respect, and I dreaded working with her again.

Once she heard my story, she spoke with conviction.

"Definitions are limitations," she said. "Do not define how she is. Every definition limits reality, perpetuating the vicious cycle that you are in."

I paused, reflecting. "So, what do you think I should do?"

"Focus on your own work, not her. She's acting in the way that is natural to her. She *knows* no other way. From everything you've told me, it sounds like she was probably abused when she was younger."

I blinked. It made a lot of sense, and everything I'd read on abuse said that it was cyclical. Children who are abused often become the abusers later on. With this new perspective, I thanked her, and a short time later she stood up.

"This is my stop. Good luck, Andrew."

"Thanks." I smiled back.

"Remember, definitions are limitations. Focus on what *you* have to do."

"I will."

As she walked off the bus, I recalled her words again and again. What *did* I have to do, really? The sequel to *The Truth Beyond the Sky* was the most important thing to me. Everything else felt secondary. When dealing with Matangi, I would focus on my work, and if she continued to have a negative attitude, then I might have to find a new environment, even if it was less comfortable or provided less flexibility.

Either way, I *would* move forward. If I held a positive attitude, the universe would give me a positive reflection.

Something would manifest. I felt that truth deep within me.

The following weekend proved to be less stressful than I had anticipated. As usual, I photographed the new developments in the Community, cleaned up the kitchen, swept and vacuumed the common area, and continued with my many web assignments. One of my favorite parts about that weekend was seeing the little pineapples that Wayne and Anne-Marie had planted. They were smaller than baseballs and pretty adorable.

Then the cat died.

In a reed basket near the kitchen, I found the black cat upside down with its eyes half open, utterly motionless as it exposed a small sore to the open air. For some reason, I felt that Matangi would want documentation of when the cat died, so I took some photos, approaching it as quietly as I could.

It still didn't respond, although it did smell. I sighed at the thought of having to dig a hole for the poor creature, deciding to leave it undisturbed for a while.

On our call that day, Matangi and I talked about many things, including what iPad she should get for the Community. She wanted the volunteers to be more responsive, and I was happy to guide her through the available options. She'd never realized that Apple offered refurbished models for a significant discount, and that put her in a good mood for the rest of the call.

Afterward, I walked back into the kitchen area and almost had a heart attack when I saw the black cat stretch out and walk away, as if nothing unusual had ever happened.

CHAPTER 18

THE BLUE FEATHER

On the following Tuesday, I set aside more time to write my second book, once again finding a relatively quiet spot on the property. It had been over two weeks since I'd last written anything for my tropically-inspired sequel, and I threw myself into the work, writing over 3,000 words that afternoon.

Buoyed by this excellent progress, I was in high spirits when I stuck out my thumb later that day, bound for Cinderland once again. Although I didn't know it at the time, that was my 12th week in a row attending Taco Tuesday, a streak I would maintain for at least another four weeks.

When I arrived, I hadn't the slightest suspicion that my 12th Tuesday night would be a harbinger of changes to come. At first, the gathering itself wasn't much different from the usual celebration of island life. By that time, hearing the unrelenting drum music felt like hearing the heartbeat of the jungle itself, as natural as my own, and I reveled in the sense of connection to everything around me.

As always, we gathered for circle-time and made the ancient Om sound together. It all washed by so quickly, as so many beautiful moments in life do.

Joining in the circle always brought the magic of where we were to the forefront. In the midst of everyday life, I must admit that I forgot it sometimes, but we were all sharing an island together, the most remote population center on the entire planet, way out in the middle of the Pacific. For some reason, joining hands reminded me of this miracle, that we were all surviving out here on the wild edge of civilization.

I caught up with Johann, who I saw dancing by the fire. He was doing well, but getting weary of his house sitting gig. I gave him a little update on my relationship with Matangi and the rest of the volunteers at the Community, and he encouraged me to be patient with the situation. Something better would come along if I kept a good attitude.

Time slipped away from me that evening. My intuition told me that it was okay to stay a bit longer, and I found myself at Cinderland after 10:00 PM, later than I ever had stayed before.

"What am I thinking?" I wondered to myself as the conversations continued to flow. "How am I going to get back?"

There were only six of us left around the small circular table, with a few others scattered around the fire behind us, most in their 20s and 30s.

Lulu, a young woman who often frequented the gathering, had opened up a small container where she collected little objects, things that she felt were significant or interesting, and she showed them to us. One of them was a beautiful blue feather, small and soft.

I asked her if I could pick it up and look at it.

"Sure!" she said.

Even though it was only about two centimeters long, I couldn't stop looking at it. Seven years before, I had listened to a podcast about Huna that had come to inspire a lot of good things in my life. I remembered a lesson from the podcast about how energy flows where attention goes, and one of the exercises was about manifestation. The teacher told us to picture a blue feather in our minds. He said that a blue feather would, eventually, come into our lives if we held the intention and really believed it.

I had intended to find a blue feather for years, and while I did come across one by chance not long after I heard the podcast, it was a plastic feather, so I didn't feel I'd manifested the real thing yet. Fully seven years had passed since then, without a single blue feather in my reality. So as I stared at this small feather in my hand, all of these thoughts came flooding back to me.

"Is it a real one?" I asked. "I mean, is it from a bird?"

"Yep," she said, "I think you should have it."

I looked up to her, shock washing over me. "Are you sure?"

"Yes," she smiled. "I think I'm *supposed* to give it to you."

Unsure of what to say, I just stared at the feather blankly. The Huna teacher had been right. Even after seven years, my intention had finally come back to me. I had manifested a blue feather, and I got the strangest feeling that the island itself was sending me a message.

I carefully pocketed the feather and at last felt that it was time for me to go; and to my incredible luck, one of the six people around the table was heading my way. I would never stay so late at Cinderland ever again, but in that instance, I felt so grateful that I'd listened to my intuition and lingered for a while longer on that warm July night.

Perhaps it sounds somewhat delusional, but from then on, I felt as if, somehow, the island itself *cared* about my wellbeing. I had a new ally, and things were going to work out, even if I didn't know exactly how.

That week, a new couple joined the Community, Ivan and Marsha. I'm not sure if it was because I was distracted from hanging out with them or if it was something else, but I skipped Uncle Robert's Wednesday night market that week. In retrospect, the regular outflow of volunteers was only tolerable because they were soon replaced by new ones. Ivan and Marsha were probably the most interesting couple to volunteer during my time at the Community, ultimately providing a useful growth catalyst for us all.

To start, we clicked instantly, and sometimes it was tricky to pull myself away from socializing to go write. Still, I managed to maintain a good balance that week, writing over 2,000 words on Thursday, the day before I received a much needed perspective shift. The following day, I even managed to find time to write about a thousand words before all of us got to talking again and the plan became clear.

Put simply, Ivan and Marsha had revealed to us a few days before that they had dried psilocybin mushrooms (aka. magic mushrooms) and wanted to share some with us.

I had thought long and hard about their offer. Besides small amounts of pakalolo (the Hawaiian word for marijuana, which became legal in several more US states over the course of writing this book), I had never done anything one might consider a drug. Even from a young age, I've been exceedingly careful about what I've put into my body. I had specifically avoided tobacco of any form, and to this day I have never used it. (However, this attitude might also be related to my grandfather dying of complications from smoking.)

Perhaps that is why I had complex feelings about taking a psychedelic compound, even with the guidance of Wayne who had shared many stories about his experience with magic mushrooms and had only positive things to say about them. Sure, some of his stories involved what appeared to be elves spouting syntax from their mouths in a wild rainbow of colors, but that was his experience. Perhaps I would get to commune with dolphins. The possibilities felt endless.

I want to be abundantly clear that, in this book, I do not advocate or recommend the use of any substance, except air and water. Pretty much everything else is up to the individual; and when taking something new, one should definitely talk to one's doctor. The psilocybin found in certain mushrooms is a powerful molecule and should be used responsibly.

Initially I had second thoughts about sharing this experience publicly; however, I have strived to tell this story as honestly as possible, and I see no good reason to censor myself on this point.

What follows is my subjective experience, and I offer it to the world in the hope that readers will find it useful.

Probably due to the fact that it was the middle of the summer, the amount of volunteers on the property had reached an all time low in July. In fact, I can only recall one or two other people at the Community besides Ivan, Marsha, Wayne, Anne-Marie, myself, and Greg. So we found it relatively easy to discuss what was to be done about the nontrivial amount of dried mushrooms they had freely offered to share. Understandably, I had lots of questions. What would I see? Would I pass out? Would I get brain damage?

These were the questions I had been trying to answer via the internet for a good portion of the week, and from lots of cross-referencing of trusted sources, I grew satisfied that, as long as I had less than a couple grams, any risk was exceedingly minimal.

I learned that psilocybin was produced by more than 200 species of mushrooms, and there was strong evidence that various genera of mushrooms had been used for thousands of years in religious ceremonies, rites of passage, and initiations. There are many ancient rituals around certain psychedelics, often connected to a coming-of-age event or other initiation. In this way, such mushrooms aren't so different from ayahuasca, a plant-based compound used to produce what is often referred to as a "visionary state of mind."

Over the past few decades, interest in these ceremonies has steadily increased, and the use of psychedelic substances in psychotherapy and as treatment for depression has gained momentum across the world, including the United States.

Of course, when handling any substance, psychedelic or not, one should use it responsibly, and I had many conversations with Wayne about how we could best set things up to have a good experience with the mushrooms. He said the jungle environment was actually ideal. While in an altered state of mind, being surrounded by positive influences has a big impact on one's experience. Pretty much the only thing I didn't like about his advice was that he warned me that I might have to vomit. He stressed that if I did throw up, it was actually a good thing, and my experience would become even more vivid.

Like most people, I don't enjoy vomiting, and the thought of running to the toilet while in an altered state of mind made me nervous. Still, out of the five people there, at least three of them had used psilocybin mushrooms in the past and had reported positive experiences. Wayne himself had used them at least a half dozen times, and his confidence helped put me at ease.

We found a place to sit near the edge of the property, and Ivan opened up a small brown bag and poured out a dried substance onto a plate. Wayne had told me the mushrooms could come in many forms, and I was surprised to learn that Ivan's mushrooms had been partially ground into a brown powder, with a few larger chunks that could have been stems. Wayne confirmed what I'd asked for: just a gram, which everyone agreed was a very small dose, even for a first timer.

He measured out a gram and gave himself and Anne-Marie about a gram and a half each. Greg, Ivan, and Marsha followed, eating the powder in a single bite with a silver spoon we'd got from the kitchen.

I glanced down to the powder in my spoon. Before I took it, I closed my eyes and inhaled deeply, listening carefully to my intuition. I felt no hint of menace or danger. If I had, I wouldn't have proceeded. This day was going to be a growth experience, I decided, and ate the powder.

To my surprise, it tasted like dry cacao, the precursor to chocolate. I swallowed it, feeling almost as if I'd eaten a small amount of sawdust. Then I took a big drink of water and sat down. Immediately, I felt like something about the situation was a bit silly, and I paid close attention to my surroundings.

For a surprisingly long time, nothing at all happened. I drank more water and talked to Wayne, who said it would take some time. After all, I hadn't had that much, anyway. Then my stomach grumbled, and I felt vaguely odd. Across from me, Greg was already chuckling to himself.

Another minute passed. There was no mistaking it. My stomach was churning, no doubt unsure of what to do with this unprecedented type of molecule. For as long as I can remember, I've had a sensitive stomach, so I wasn't surprised at all. But this was a growth experience, and my friends supported me. If I had to run over to the bushes and vomit in the jungle, then I would. Either way, I would be okay.

Time felt weird.

I looked down to the green at my feet. The ground was moving. The pattern itself was swirling in a rather bizarre and beautiful way; yet another part of my brain knew that the ground wasn't moving at all.

Interesting, I thought. It must be working.

"Wayne," I said, "I think the ground is cycling through colors or something. Do you see that?"

He chuckled.

"Yeah, man! Just take it easy and enjoy yourself, okay?"

My stomach tightened, and I felt sicker.

Zarking fardwarks! This whole experience is going to be tainted because I have a sensitive stomach, I thought to myself. Stupid genes. Stupid stomach.

For some reason, I had trouble looking away from the ground, and I felt my sense of time blur around me. I took another drink of water and coughed. The water seemed to make my stomach even more upset.

"Wayne, I feel like I have to throw up." I turned to him, and his face seemed more vivid than before, crisp.

He said something about how it would pass in time. I just had to stay calm.

I looked up to Greg who was laughing quietly to himself, seemingly in his own little world. I wasn't surprised. I looked over to Anne-Marie, who was talking to Wayne about how obvious something was.

"Yes!" she said, "It makes so much sense."

"What makes sense?" I asked.

She laughed, saying how it was a long story but perhaps she would explain later.

The colors on the ground were swirling in bright patterns. It was as if the ground itself were made of something between a solid and a liquid, both yet neither.

I looked over to my hands and realized I was gripping the lawn chair tightly. I consciously relaxed my hands, taking a fresh new breath. Then I was going to throw up. There wasn't much I could do about it anymore. "Wayne, how long does your stomach usually stay upset?"

"Take a deep breath. It'll pass. And if it doesn't, it's okay to throw up. We're in the jungle," he chuckled. "Don't worry."

I inhaled, struggling to calm my stomach.

"Andrew," Ivan called out, "can you come over here?"

He was standing farther away from the group than he had been before, and I carefully got up and approached him, feeling my balance waver as I walked over.

"Hey man, what's up? Are you okay?" I asked ironically.

"Are *you* okay?" he said. "Do you want to go for a short walk? I think it might help you."

"Uh," I paused. "Yeah. Yeah, I think that sounds like a good idea. Where do you want to go?"

"Let's just head down the road. I'll lead the way."

"Okay."

On some roads, I might have been concerned about traffic, but this particular road had about one car every blue moon so I wasn't worried.

We followed the road in silence at first, just looking up at the fractal trees around us. As I glanced up at the towering albizia trees around us, their branch structure was simplified. And in this simplified way of seeing them, the fractal pattern of their growth was obvious to me. Each branch sprouted as part of a mathematical formula that the tree was running, encoded by its DNA. The tree branches couldn't help but grow in this pattern. Each smaller part of the branch had the same pattern as the larger part, lavished with an abundance of green all around, and I was humbled by this new perspective of its beauty.

"Do you see it? The trees are fractals!" I said.

He nodded, agreeing with me.

"This island really is special, you know. I've only been here for a few months, and I already love it." I turned to him. "So why did you pick Hawaii to visit if you didn't know anyone here? This is your first time here, right?"

"Yep." He nodded. "Well, Andrew, to be honest, earlier this year we had a close friend pass away. He was pretty young, and it was a shock to us."

"Oh my gosh. I'm sorry."

"His passing kind of woke us up to how short life is. Marsha and I have always felt drawn to Hawaii, and when he died, we knew we had to come here... while we still could. You don't know how long you have, Andrew, and you need to do what's in your heart while you can."

His words hit me hard. The truth of his story was like a gut punch, and I swallowed, trying to digest it all.

"You're right," I inhaled deeply. "Well, you made the right choice in coming while you could. This island is the most magical place I've ever been to, and I've been all over the place."

Somehow we were only halfway down the road, even though it felt like we'd been walking for an hour. Of course, time dilation was a common side effect of these mushrooms. Moving ahead felt like moving through a never-ending tunnel of albizia trees, as if it had no end. But eventually, we did reach the end and turned around. Mostly, I got caught up in the stunning fractal patterns of the trees.

When we returned to the Community, I realized that my stomach felt much better after walking and thanked Ivan for inviting me to walk with him. I told him I'd come back later but I wanted to write for a while. He understood, and I headed to a private area to write on my laptop.

As I sat down, I noticed that night had fallen while I wasn't paying attention. That meant a few hours had already passed. Even so, I could feel that I was still tuned into a slightly unusual frequency of reality, and I sat down and wrote in TextEdit. What I wrote there is difficult to describe. Suffice to say, that I found myself in a dialogue with myself, and fragments of my higher self simmered through.

As I journaled, my higher self said that writing was part of my life purpose, and I felt vindicated at this realization. This higher part of me also said that I was meant to come to Hawaii.

CHAPTER 19

MEETING THE WIZARD

There once was a girl called Lilith who wore horn-rimmed glasses. She was smart, nerdy, and pretty quirky in a particular combination that was uncommon in Puna. Her boyfriend Anansi was smart and nerdy, too; and they had a unique kind of chemistry that was difficult to describe.

In addition to having a smile that instantly put me at ease, Lilith popped up in common places at uncommon times which is perhaps why I cannot recall exactly when I first met her. Most likely it was at Kehena Beach or Cinderland, quickly realizing that we moved in similar circles. I must have made a good impression, because she invited me to her birthday party the following week, giving me the address to her place, which turned out to be rather close to the Community I was staying in.

And that is how, exactly one day after using psilocybin for the first time, I met Anansi, someone who I still consider to be somewhat of a wizard.

The party proved to be trivially easy to hitchhike to, and I made sure to bring something, I think it was guacamole, to share. When I walked into the humble, pale-colored house, there was already a beautiful spread of food on the table, and almost everyone was dressed up in bright, colorful clothing. I recall Noah being there, the one I'd met at Taco Tuesday some weeks before who sounded like a book whenever he spoke. Lulu, the girl who gave me the blue feather, was also there, along with lots of other faces that I knew well but whose names I hadn't yet learned. I wished Johann or Doran could have come.

Lilith greeted me with a warm hug, graciously introducing me to some of her friends to break the ice. Nearby, people were dancing to music in the living room, but after a while I wandered over to the kitchen where Lilith and her boyfriend were talking. I'd seen Anansi at Taco Tuesday and exchanged a few words with him here and there, but we'd never had a memorable conversation before. Even though he was a few years older than me, he possessed a playful exuberance, while also having an uncommon depth to his thoughts. Somehow, I found him instantly familiar.

In addition to the bandana wrapped around his head, he had a kind of mystery wrapped around him, too. Soon, all three of us were talking, Anansi perched on a round stool in the middle of the kitchen. And as we talked, Anansi's voice grew animated as he shared how he'd gotten a new perspective on his feminine side recently. I don't recall the details of his revelation, but I'll never forget the way his eyes seemed to radiate a light of their own as he spoke. His natural charisma was unmistakable, and although I didn't know it at the time, I would learn a lot from him about the balance of the masculine and feminine in each of us.

The party ebbed and flowed, and later on some of the guests played instruments on the front porch. Soon, the party was filled with live keyboards and guitars, and the night stretched on into immeasurable time until I realized how late it was and told Lilith I had to go. Her friend asked me how far I was going and volunteered to drive me back to the Community. Even though it was only about a 10 minute drive, I was humbled at her generosity and thanked her profusely.

When I returned to the Community a bit later, I couldn't get the image of Lilith and Anansi the Wizard out of my head. Their relationship dynamic seemed much more charged than most of the couples I'd met in Puna. What was different about them? Perhaps I would learn if I was patient.

The next day began with a call from Matangi early that morning. She wanted me to photograph more of the grounds, and as she said that, I realized that I had the unenviable job of telling her that the iPad she'd ordered had turned out to be a lemon. Earlier in the week, when it had arrived in the mail, Wayne and I had booted it up, dismayed to find that it only showed black and white lines across its screen. However, I had anticipated this conversation with Matangi and had preemptively called Apple to tell them that we'd gotten a dud. They helped me ship the old one back, and a new one was already on its way.

"I'm sorry, Matangi," I said. "We got a dud. Sometimes these things happen."

"Yes, but is it covered by the warranty?"

"Yes, all refurbished Apple products have the same warranty as their new products. I already called them, actually. We sent back the old one; the new one is on its way. I took care of it."

"Oh." She sounded surprised and relieved. "Thank you for taking care of that, Andrew."

"Of course."

For the rest of the weekend, I got more work done on the website, finished up some new graphics, and post-processed many more photos that I'd been taking of the property. Thankfully, that weekend went pretty smoothly, and I hoped that it was a sign of things to come.

As I said before, the middle of the summer was a nadir in terms of how many people were at the Community. It was an oddly quiet time. Matangi was handling volunteer and guest bookings while she was travelling. But besides that, Wayne, Anne-Marie, and I were basically running the place ourselves. We kept the place clean, maintained the gardens, checked in and trained new volunteers, and held regular meetings, among other things. The situation forced Wayne and Anne-Marie, who had been sharing a shift before, to have their own separate work shifts; so they were on the lookout for volunteers who might want to stay on a bit longer and take on more responsibilities in exchange for staying at the Community for free.

As one can imagine, this shortage of long-term volunteers forced us to rely on each other even more, and all three of us formed an even closer bond of friendship that summer. Although they were in their early 20s, I learned that they'd already been on plenty of adventures, living on the east coast, Arizona, and California. They'd come to the Big Island to get a change of pace. And over the summer, Wayne and I had deep and refreshingly honest conversations about life, the universe, and everything. Whenever I was feeling down, Wayne noticed. And over time, I showed him some of the negative messages Matangi would send me. It didn't take long before Wayne realized that Matangi did not treat all of the volunteers equally.

As Wayne and Anne's obsession with *The Walking Dead* waned, we would often watch movies and other shows after dinner on their little white MacBook. We even had a streak of watching the reboot of *Battlestar Galactica*. Other times, I'd recommend a movie they'd never seen before, and we'd have engaging discussions about it afterwards. Wayne was especially impressed by the film *Contact* with Jodie Foster.

Although the age difference between us was noticeable in certain contexts, Wayne had a worldly wisdom about him that often made me forget the fact that he was younger than I was. And Anne-Marie had an innate spunk and resiliency that belied her years.

Without them, I'm not sure what I would have done. I cannot state that strongly enough. Wayne's calming influence was particularly helpful as I continued to write 2,000 to 4,000 words per week for the sequel to *The Truth Beyond the Sky*, balanced with my island explorations and my Community duties.

And when Greg left just a few weeks after the summer nadir, it hit me once again just how transient that part of the island was. I would miss his calming influence, too, not to mention his excellent cooking. There were rougher roads ahead.

CHAPTER 20

THE UNFORGETTABLE WEEK

By late July, I felt the itch to explore Hilo more deeply.

On Monday, I called up Rob, and he said he'd be happy to host me Wednesday night, although he warned me that a small tropical depression was heading toward the island. I checked the radar, and it didn't look too bad. Although I didn't have a specific plan for my next Hilo trip, I hoped to finally make it up to Mauna Kea, the highest point on the island; but to do that, I would need help and a bit of luck.

Tuesday turned out to be a warm-up for that unforgettable week. Johann and I planned to hike out onto the Kalapana lava field and find the Cave of Refuge, a hidden cave that opened up to a spectacular view of infinite ocean. We'd been talking about it for weeks, and I was glad that we finally had a concrete plan to go out and actually find it. He also asked me if it was okay if he brought a friend along.

"Of course," I said. "Any friend of yours must be pretty cool."

Later that morning, I arrived at the small complex of buildings known as Uncle Robert's—the same place that the night market was held every Wednesday evening. We waited for a few minutes for Johann's friend Skeeter to show up, and when he did, he handed Johann a small book, the same book that he'd been talking about ever since I'd met him: *Wise Secrets of Aloha*.

Johann thanked Skeeter for returning it and said that I should borrow it next.

"Definitely," I said. "You've told me so much about how you love it. I'll definitely read it."

"Awesome," he said. "I'll give it to you when we get back from the hike."

We began, following a narrow red cinder trail that marked the fastest way over the lava rock to a small black sand beach that bordered the lava field. The beach might have been a good place to swim, except that its rip current was even worse than Kehena beach. Still, it was a beautiful place to visit, and we stood on the black sand for a few minutes, enjoying the contrast of the white waves as they crashed against the smooth black stones that collected in patches around the beach.

A short time later we stepped back up to the shelf of black lava rock that rose about a meter above the beach and followed the edge of the island, toward a small patch of greenery in the distance. Johann said that the entrance to the Cave of Refuge was within that green oasis. The only problem was, that was all we knew. None of us had ever been there before. All we knew were stories. Even so, we were determined to track the entrance down. How hard could it be?

On a lava field, accurately judging distance can be tricky, and as we followed the sloping lava rock as it undulated upslope and downslope, the trees didn't seem to grow much closer. We talked to pass the time, eventually reaching the green area an hour later, a raised oasis of trees that the lava hadn't hit called a kīpuka (kee-poo-ka), and then it took us a good while to find a decent path to climb up onto it. Once we got on the kīpuka itself, I was surprised at how thick the bushes and trees grew, and we pushed our way through the thick undergrowth with white hot determination. We would find the entrance, or at the very least have a good story to tell later.

And then, I saw it.

Below a layer of bushes, I noticed a hollow space. Excitement bubbled up within me, and I pushed the bushes aside, noticing a long crevice that reached down into the darkness. I followed it ahead, noticing that it grew wider the farther I went. Then it was wide enough that someone might be able to fit inside. Had I found it?

Johann leaned over and stuck his head inside.

"Well?" I asked. "Does it look like an entrance at all?"

He pulled his head back out from the thick undergrowth, furrowing his eyebrows. "Sorry. I don't think so, man. It doesn't look like it goes anywhere."

I sighed, hopelessness threatening me. We agreed that the real entrance would look more like a cave and less like a crevice. After all, every story we'd heard mentioned an actual cave entrance, not a crevice.

We continued onward, soon reaching a boundary where the forest atop the kīpuka was so thick that we couldn't penetrate it. Perhaps it was within the thicket? But how could we reach it?

In the end, we headed back down, off of the kīpuka to a small plateau that provided a good view of the waves crashing against the jet-black boulders below. After the frustration of being unable to find the cave, I found the sound of the ocean waves soothing. More information would come to me, as it had a habit of doing. And when I knew more, I would return to this place and find it.

By then, it was well past noon, and Johann and Skeeter were getting thirsty, so we began the trek back. Over an hour later, we reached the Kalapana Café and got some drinks, and I noticed a large, circular mural painted on the side of the building. A sea turtle, clown fish, rays, and coral were beautifully depicted, a huge volcano erupting behind them all.

When we got back to the parking lot, Johann handed me a small book, bringing a smile to my face.

"So this is it, huh?" I read the cover, which was dominated by a photo of a pink *Hibiscus* flower:

WISE SECRETS OF ALOHA
Learn and Live the Sacred Art of Lomilomi

The book was surprisingly thin, only about 150 pages.

I turned it over and read the description, which referred to the author, Harry Jim, as a Kahuna of Lomilomi, Keeper of the Deep Mysteries. It went on to describe lomilomi as an ancient healing tradition, a set of four basic techniques that open us up to healing in the body and spirit. And, as I would learn over the coming months, the concept of Aloha was a key part of that healing, too.

I looked up to Johann. "Thank you! I can't wait to read it."

"Of course." He smiled warmly back to me. "It's a really powerful book. I think you'll enjoy it."

Carefully, I stowed the book in my brown daypack. Skeeter said that he had to get going, and thanked us for a good hike.

"Well, we did our best. See you later!"

He waved and drove away, and we walked over to the intersection where the road headed north again, toward Pahoa.

"What do you want to do now?" Johann asked, the sun glinting off of his blond hair.

"I don't know. Is there anything else cool around here that's not too tricky to hitchhike to?"

"Have you been to the painted church? It's pretty cool."

"Actually, I've been meaning to go there!" I said, feeling suddenly very aligned with this new idea. "Are we pretty close?"

"Yeah. Probably 20 minutes up the road."

A smile spread across my face. "Let's check it out!"

It didn't take long for us to get a ride up to the small church, a small mint-colored building with a steep roof and a depiction of Christ on a cross high above the entrance. A painted sign beside the road read:

STAR OF THE SEA
Painted Church
Mass This Friday
4 00 PM

We headed up the five concrete steps to two wide doors, painted in white trim, which had been left open. And as I stepped inside, thousands of details flooded into my eyes.

True to its name, nearly every surface inside the church was lovingly painted. Above a lectern in the center, depictions of angels holding heavenly banners formed an arch over a carved representation of Christ nailed to a wooden cross with the letters INRI painted above his head, an abbreviation of a Latin phrase which means "Jesus the Nazarene, King of the Jews."

More arches had been painted onto the wall behind the cross, creating a forced-perspective effect that made the space behind the lectern seem to go on farther than it actually did.

Nearby, I noticed historical paintings on the walls, depicting Father Damien De Veuster's first church, which had been built just a few kilometers south of there. Father Damien himself was also depicted, wearing a white habit around his neck.

Later, I learned that he was originally from Belgium. He'd spent 16 years caring for the sick in a leper colony on the nearby Island of Molokai, and became recognized as Saint Damien of Molokai. In fact, he was only the tenth person in the United States to be recognized as a saint by the Catholic Church.

As I read about the remarkable service and care that he provided to the lepers, I felt utterly moved at his sacrifice, especially since he himself died of leprosy in 1889.

The painted church had a remarkable history of its own, having been threatened by advancing lava flows more than once.

And in 1990, the entire building had to be moved north when a lava flow overran Kalapana village.

It was a miracle that the church had survived multiple earthquakes, tropical storms, and lava flows. And as we soaked in the beauty of the painted church, Johann told me about how some Hawaiians believed that Jesus's spirit had come to the islands long ago.

Johann's words piqued my interest.

"You know," he said as he admired the arching banners above us, held aloft by angels with golden wings, "some people even believe that Jesus's bones were brought *here* to the islands. And the bones—"

He abruptly stopped, and I looked over to him in surprise. I had been hanging on his every word.

"What?" I asked. "What about the bones?"

Johann remained silent.

"What is it? Is something wrong?"

"I should stop there," he said. "The person who told me this might not be happy about me talking about it. I've probably already said too much."

"Okay," I said. "Yeah, I don't want you to say anything you don't feel comfortable talking about."

I swallowed and looked back outside, sensing a new tension in the room.

"Are you okay?" I asked, turning back to him.

He shook off the tension. "Yeah, I'm fine."

"You wanna go? I think I've seen everything."

"Yeah, let's go."

And as we walked out, I got the feeling that I would find out more about that story when, and if, I was ready. It would be years before I found out where the story originally came from and was granted permission to share part of it in this book.

The following day was a Wednesday, and I spent that morning packing a few things in my daypack before hitchhiking over to the four-way intersection that was the launching point for so many of my adventures that summer.

When I'd talked to Rob on the phone, I'd shared how much I wanted to go up to Mauna Kea, and he mentioned that a young woman named Rita was also couchsurfing at his place that night. He said that perhaps she would be interested.

After getting dropped off near the bay front, I made the familiar trek farther into town to Rob's house. But when I arrived, Rita wasn't there, so I headed out to explore more and grab some food at the store.

When I returned later that evening to make a quick dinner, I finally got to meet her. She was sweet and seemed almost as excited about Mauna Kea as I was, but she would have to check with the friends she was travelling with and see what they thought. And we agreed to talk more about it in the morning.

Thursday was August 1, the beginning of a month that would turn out to be a time of great endings and beginnings for me.

That morning, Rita and I spent a light meal discussing our plans. She had checked with her friends. They would join us in a separate vehicle, but they were really excited, too. It was really happening. We would drive to the top of Mauna Kea.

"No, you won't, I'm afraid," Rob interjected.

I turned to him. "Why not?"

"Because Rita has a rental car," he said, "and no rental car company will insure a car past the Mauna Kea visitor center. You won't be able to get all the way to the top."

I furrowed my eyebrows. "None of the rental companies?"

He nodded. "The rule is specifically written into the contract of every rental car company on the island. And it's a really steep road to the top. You have to have a vehicle with 4-wheel drive to make it up there safely."

"Crap."

I took another bite of the pasta, reflecting on our options.

"Wait a minute, what if we *hitchhiked* the rest of the way?"

Rita pursed her lips. "Maybe. Have you done it before?"

I laughed. "Done it? It's my primary means of transportation right now. People are friendly here, and they usually ask good questions. Sometimes I think they just want a good story, and I have plenty of stories to share. Anyway, they seem happy after they pick me up."

She smiled. "Well, if you're so confident about it, I guess we can try. We'll see how much traffic is actually heading up there once we get to the visitor center."

"Of course. But I think we've got a great shot."

And so we took Route 200, known locally as the Saddle Road, up the mountain toward the visitor center, eventually making a sharp right turn onto the Mauna Kea access road. There was much less vegetation up there, and we passed large, dormant volcanic cones on our way in.

After following a narrow winding road, we finally reached a small complex of buildings and a parking lot that was flanked by two large mounds to either side. We got out and breathed the crisp, thin air. Her two friends were already there and met us at the parking lot. The only problem was, the sun was setting, and I was all too familiar with how fast one could run out of daylight at just 19.5° above the equator.

I looked around, finding signs posted where the road continued upward to the summit. There was even a large speed bump to encourage drivers to really think about their choice before heading onward. Still, there were enough drivers heading up that I felt we had a good shot at hitching it.

"Ready?" I asked her.

"Okay, let's try it."

At first, all four of us stood together, trying to hitch up as one group; but after a few minutes, I realized that the strategy needed some improvement. A single driver probably wouldn't have room for all four of us, so I suggested we split into two groups. Everyone agreed, and Rita and I stuck out our thumbs, ready to beam powerful smiles to oncoming drivers.

I'm not sure if it was the fact that hitchhiking was outside of Rita's comfort zone or that the thinness of the air was affecting our brains, but as we waited for a car to head up to the summit, we just started giggling to ourselves. This passed the time for a couple minutes until, to our relief, a huge pickup truck wheeled up to us and stopped. Inside I could see a middle-aged couple.

"Need a ride?" the woman smiled down to us.

I smiled up to her in return. "Yes! We would love one. We've never been to the top before, and our two friends really want to see it. We only have rental cars, so—"

"Oh, of course! Come on in!"

Rita and I swung open the large black doors of the truck and slid in, her two friends running up behind us.

Soon, all six of us were heading up to the top of Mauna Kea, the tallest point on the entire island; and I had trouble pulling my eyes away from the menagerie of colors that was growing in the sky. The clouds were bunched up like fluffy white pillows that stretched on forever, bathed in the ever-changing mango hues of the sunset. We took some sharp turns through narrow passes until I saw a strange shape in front of the clouds: a dark triangle looming up from the horizon. Just as I made a mental note to ask about it later, we turned and the steep rocks blocked it from my view.

We turned again, and I saw a small island of rock poke above the layer of clouds, splashed orange and red by the setting sun. It would be close, but it looked like we would make it in time for the sunset. From this new perspective, I saw a winding road far below, the lower part of the access road we'd been on just a few minutes before, and beyond it was a vanilla sky.

After another turn, a collection of white domes came into view, massive telescopes peppering the rocky landscape; and behind them, the mysterious triangular peak loomed once again, a perfect geometric shape rising up into the sky. And as the sun grew ever lower on the horizon, the colors grew deeper.

In the distance, smaller rocky peaks poked up above the cloud layer, and it all felt like a scene from another planet.

At last, our drivers found a parking lot and came to a gentle stop. "You guys just let us know when you're ready to go, okay?" the woman said, turning around. "We're up here to enjoy the sunset, too."

"Sounds great! Thanks again. We really appreciate the ride."

I zipped my jacket up partway and cracked the door open, freezing air blasting into my face. "Yikes!"

Stepping down from the vehicle, I zipped my jacket up all the way and tried to find my footing on the cinder gravel. The air stung my lungs at first, but it had a strange, almost euphoric quality to it. I looked out and noticed a tall mound downslope from us that some people had climbed up to, lit afire by the setting sun.

Beside it was the mysterious triangular peak once again. I stared at it for some time, marveling at its geometric perfection, almost as if someone had taken a protractor and made a dark triangle in the sky.

And suddenly, I realized what it was.

Of course! It was the shadow that Mauna Kea cast onto the clouds behind it. Only occurring during sunrise and sunset, this shadow was a perfect geometric wonder, and because of its vast size, it was easy to mistake it for another mountain in the far distance, only much darker.

As it dawned on me, I felt giddy at the thought that I was standing on one of the most remarkable mountains on the planet. At 4,207 meters above sea level, Mauna Kea is superb for astronomy and a rare sight to behold. In fact, when measured from the bottom of the ocean, Mauna Kea is over 10,000 meters tall, making it the tallest mountain on Earth, at least, if one includes mountains that start on the ocean floor. (For comparison, Mount Everest is 8,848 meters tall.)

I walked over to Rita who was taking photos of the unending clouds that stretched off into the distance, and I pointed out how the nearby observatories appeared bright orange in the final light of the day. I had seen photos of these telescopes on the internet, massive silver and white domes that peered deeply into the cosmos, but I never imagined I would actually get to stand so close to them.

Maybe it was the cold, but a minute later I realized that I needed to use the restroom. Would they let me use one even if I wasn't an employee? I walked up to the nearest dome and pushed the door open, walking down a white-tiled hall. I ran into a woman wearing an ID tag and asked if there was a restroom I could use. She smiled and pointed down a hall to the right.

Inside the observatory, it was easy to forget that I was at such great elevation, and I wished that I'd known in advance when we would have arrived. I might have scheduled a tour. Then again, such was the trade-off of hitchhiking. It may save money and provide flexibility, especially when rental cars are forbidden in certain places, but it can be tricky to plan around.

When I got back outside, the sun was just a few degrees above the horizon, and farther down I saw a pair of almost identical white structures that I would later learn were the Keck Observatory domes, both of which are among the largest currently active astronomical telescopes on the planet.

Rita asked me if I could take a picture of her in front of the sun before it finally set. I estimated that we had about a minute before that happened, so we'd have to be quick.

"Yes, definitely!"

I snapped a few photos of her, and she did the same for me, taking the photo just moments before the bottom edge of the sun's disc, which appeared paler up there, touched the pastel, cloudy horizon.

Throughout all of these moments, we couldn't stop smiling. We had made it. We had taken a risk, and it had paid off. And I spent the rest of the sunset photographing the white disc of the sun as it sank below the silver-lined clouds.

Once the sun had set, I found my attention drawn to the wealth of observatories all around me. I counted at least six or seven huge white domes in varying sizes, most perched atop their own mound, looking out on an unbroken sea of puffy, periwinkle clouds below.

I turned around, and the generous couple who had driven us up were strolling back over to their truck. Taking this as a signal, I followed them back over to where they'd parked. They were ready to go, and we felt similarly. They said the visitor center below usually did a guided star watch, and if we left soon, we would arrive in time.

The drive down felt much longer, and after the freezing air of the summit, we all welcomed the warmth of the truck. Roughly a half hour later, we found ourselves back at the visitor center parking lot and got out, thanking the couple profusely for making our dream of reaching the summit come true.

I looked over to the visitor center, my eyes drawn to a strange red light within. And when I stepped inside, I realized that every light source in the room was deep red, no doubt to preserve everyone's night vision for the star watch that would soon begin. Inside, I found every kind of astronomical gift one could think of: shirts, posters, rotating discs that indicate what stars will be rising depending on the date and time, and much more. They even had freeze-dried astronaut ice cream.

Eventually, people shuffled outside, and I followed them, noticing that some large telescopes had been set up in the sandy area between the visitor center and the road. A man introduced himself as Bergmann and mentioned that he was part of the West Hawaii Astronomy Club.

He pulled out a bright green laser pointer that seemed somehow familiar and pointed out some of the constellations above us. Surprisingly, the small laser was easily visible in the sky above, making a green dot that fluttered around the stars. Using the pointer, Bergmann taught us about the summer triangle, a collection of three bright stars that are only easy to see in the summer. He also pointed out Ursa Major and several other prominent stars, until he finally concluded his tour and said that the telescopes were each aimed at an astronomical point of interest that was currently visible in the night sky.

In moments, people formed long lines in front of the telescopes which ranged from one to over two meters long. I got in one line, and after a short wait I saw the brilliant yellow disc of Saturn, haloed in its thick, ancient rings. In fact, that night felt like a smorgasbord of astronomical delights. Next, I saw Messier 7, an open cluster of stars in the constellation of

Scorpius. Although it's estimated to be over 900 light-years distant, its bright stars looked like shimmering specks of white sand floating in the blackness. They seemed oddly close, like I could reach out and touch them, if only I knew how.

Yet without a doubt, the most memorable object I saw that night was Messier 51, which is actually a full-blown spiral galaxy just like our own Milky Way. First cataloged by French astronomer Charles Messier in 1773, the galaxy has come to be known as the Whirlpool Galaxy and has become so famous that most people have seen at least one picture of it.

Once my eye got focused on the object, I had trouble believing what I was seeing. There it was, an entire spiral galaxy right in my field of vision. Being somewhat of an astronomy geek myself, I'd seen this galaxy in photos hundreds of times before, but to actually see it through a telescope was a rare honor.

The astronomer directing that particular scope mentioned that it was so incredibly faint that the telescope was enhancing the brightness of the image somewhat, but it was indeed the Whirlpool Galaxy. Just as I'd seen in photos countless times before, it was attracting stars from the smaller galaxy to the right, what I later learned was called M51B.

The man overseeing the telescope said that the galaxy was so distant he had to use the telescope's built-in computer to continually adjust its alignment to correct for the Earth's rotation. Since the galaxy is over 15 million light-years from Earth, it was easily the most distant object I've ever had the honor of seeing with my own eyes.

Even after all that, there was still one final wonder that I saw before the night came to a close.

I got in line for the one telescope I hadn't looked through yet, the largest of the four that had been set out. Of course, it was

Bergmann's. I didn't know it yet, but he'd pointed his huge machine at the grand finale of the night.

"Are you familiar with the Pillars of Creation?" he asked when I reached the front of the line.

I blinked. "You mean, the star eggs? Where some stars are being born?"

"I guess you could say that. Come look."

I pressed my left eye up to the soft rubber of the eyepiece and saw a strange hazy shape that I had trouble focusing on at first.

"See the dark V-shaped object?" he asked. "Those are the Pillars of Creation."

I squinted, just barely discerning the tall outlines of massive clouds that formed part of the Eagle Nebula. The color was muted compared to the photos I'd seen, but it was certainly the right shape. Within those immense pillars of gas and dust, I imagined the wealth of new stars forming, even in that moment, from the debris of ancient supernovae. At over 6,500 light-years from Earth, the sight of the Pillars of Creation was hauntingly beautiful, the dark inner portions of the nebulae forming a V shape from our particular latitude, so distant that if I so much as breathed on the telescope, its image vibrated with my breath.

That evening we left humbled by the ineffable beauty of the cosmos, and so ended the unforgettable week.

It wouldn't be my last.

The following week, Rita left the island, and I never saw her again. But by then I was getting used to it. Such were the ways of life when living on a tropical island.

CHAPTER 21

MEETING SELENA

After visiting the top of Mauna Kea, I sensed a shift within me.

Perhaps a sign of a new chapter in my own journey, I felt somehow that new, hitherto unreachable horizons were opening up to me. And I began to find a good rhythm between spending time working at the Community, enjoying weekly events around Puna, and exploring the sights around Hilo. It felt good to be in motion when my spirit moved me and then in a quiet place in the Community when I needed solitude.

I hitchhiked more than ever that month, and Johann and I spent more time together as we realized that we had lots of shared interests, spanning from video editing to web design. He had some good company ideas, too, but unfortunately I never saw those ideas manifest in the short time I knew him.

He had been house sitting for another homeowner in Puna and had invited me to stay over that week and hang out, assuring me that he'd made sure it was okay with the owner. The idea excited me because, like the Community, the house was nestled in the middle of the jungle. It even had water catchment tanks and solar power.

But there was one major difference from the Community: the house was elevated above the ground, with a beautiful kitchen and a lovely view. Plus, it had modern windows and not just open holes covered in screens that were a common substitute for windows in Puna. In short, it was a real house.

We planned to meet at the house in the evening, and I spent the afternoon enjoying my day off, lounging around Pahoa town and enjoying a good lunch at Island Naturals market.

When I noticed the sun getting low in the sky, I walked down to my usual launching point: the four-way intersection that led to all points east, north, and west. I walked over to a certain corner so I would be in the best position to head in a direction I didn't often head. On this uncommon side, I noticed a woman sitting on a guard rail that bordered the road, strumming a small ukulele and singing to herself.

I blinked, startled at the passion and sweetness with which she played. When she raised her eyes to me, I felt my chest tense slightly. She was more lovely than any woman I'd ever met on the island. I took a deep breath to calm myself, telling myself that she most certainly couldn't be as angelic as she was currently appearing. After all, it was nearly dusk. It must have been some trick of the light, I told myself, some taste of the magic hour that only occurs at sunrise and sunset that was making her look more attractive than was actually possible.

Perhaps.

"You sing well," I blabbered, feeling unsure of how to start the conversation. "How long have you been on the island? I don't think I've seen you before."

She thanked me for the compliment and explained that she'd been on the island for a few months but had jumped back and forth a few times. As she talked, I found myself enjoying every little movement she made, and I steadied myself. I had experienced this phenomenon before, and I suddenly felt a little stupid. Wasn't I too old to have such a strong attraction to someone right when I met them? I had to keep my cool.

We continued to talk, and I grew more and more intrigued by her. I could tell that she was a few years older than me, but she had a childlike playfulness and a quick smile that felt like a breath of fresh air. I introduced myself, and she replied in kind.

Her name was Selena, and just as our conversation had really started to flow, Heartsong lumbered up, holding a ukulele of his own, and said hello to her. Apparently, she knew him, but I sensed only a friendly interaction. Besides, I got the feeling that she didn't usually go for guys in their late 40s.

So when they were strumming ukuleles together a short time later, I didn't feel threatened like some guys would have in my position. Honestly, the only emotion I felt was annoyance that our fun conversation had been sidetracked. It turned out that all three of us were heading in the same direction, so unless we got lucky and a pickup truck stopped, we would probably be separated. The reality was that most folks in Puna simply weren't willing to pick up three people at the same time.

Yet in a surprisingly short amount of time, a car pulled over to the side of the road. There was already someone in the passenger seat, but the driver said that all three of us would fit in the back; and we filed in, realizing that yes, we did fit. (We would have fit better if Heartsong had been a bit smaller, but a free ride was a free ride.) Anyway, I wasn't going to complain. The only problem was that Selena and Heartsong were chatting up a storm, and my stop would be the first one.

If I wanted to see her again, I would need to ask her for her number, and I waited for a natural break in the conversation, some elegant natural pause when I would ask. Yes, there would be a good time. Any minute now.

The driver pulled over to the side of the road.

"Okay, this is where you said you wanted to be dropped off, right?" the driver said.

"Uh, yes," I hesitated. I considered asking her in that moment, but I didn't want the question to feel forced. Before I knew it, I waved goodbye to both Heartsong and Selena and was standing on the side of the road, alone.

In hindsight, I was so nervous that I would say something stupid that I allowed it to freeze my thinking, and as I walked into Leilani Estates, my heart was filled with a strange mixture of frustration with myself and sheer excitement about the person I'd just met. I would see her again, I told myself.

I had to.

As I walked deeper into Leilani Estates where Johann was staying, I couldn't help but feel sillier and sillier for not asking Selena for her phone number, and my mind jumped between extremes. I imagined that I would definitely see her again soon.

After all, Puna is only 1,300 square kilometers, and although it had a population of about 40,000, it felt much smaller. The circle of people who actually hitchhiked was only a small fraction of that. We were more visible than the average person.

But what if that was it? What if I didn't run into her again? What if, by not seizing the opportunity to ask for her phone number, I had doomed myself to never seeing her again? Doomed myself to forever wondering what could have been?

The daylight was almost extinguished, leaving me to walk down the narrow unpaved road in the dark, as all of these thoughts swirled around in my mind.

I oscillated between a sense that I would see her again and a certainty that I wouldn't.

When I reached the end of the road, I realized that I hadn't seen the address for the house anywhere and turned around. The sign must have been in the undergrowth. In the end, I had to use my iPod as a flashlight to find the small address painted on a sign nailed to a tree, partially covered by leaves.

The driveway curved off deeper into the jungle, and a short time later I came upon a tall house standing in the middle of a clearing in the forest, ensconced in the shadows created by the final glow of dusk.

I found a stairwell that headed up to an elevated porch and knocked on the door. Johann opened it in moments, a big smile spreading across his face, and he gave me a great bear hug.

That evening, he'd prepared a delicious vegetable soup, and I thanked him heartily for inviting me to stay over, telling him that his support came at the perfect time. I told him about Selena, and he assured me that of course I would see her again. Puna wasn't that big, and he was quite positive that I would see her again soon. He felt that strongly.

We spent the rest of the evening catching up, encouraging each other, and telling stories. I found the overall environment of the house to be one of the most comfortable spaces I'd come across in a while, and drifted off to sleep in the living room guest bed that he had graciously prepared for me.

The next morning, I was abruptly awoken by a loud *cock-a-doodle-doo!*

The bird was still far off, but it was close enough to wake me up, and I got the feeling there was no escaping jungle fowl while living on the Big Island.

On Tuesday, I did what I always did: I went to Cinderland. And as I rode past the lava field on the way, I intended that she would be there. After all, most people who hitchhiked found their way to Cinderland sooner or later. At least, it seemed that way. I would help make delicious tacos; then I would turn around; and she'd be there.

Of course, when I got there she was nowhere to be found.

Anansi the Wizard was there, though, and I talked to him for a while before I went over to the food table to help chop some vegetables. I asked him why his girlfriend Lilith never came, and he smiled and shrugged, finally saying that he didn't think it was her scene.

Nearby, I ran into Noah, which wasn't a huge surprise since he lived at Cinderland at the time. Tonight, he was shirtless, but the more I spoke with Noah, the more I realized that he had a childlike heart filled with nothing but kindness. If I had ever seen him hurt a fly, I would have been shocked. And I never did.

I asked him if I could have a tour of the east side of Cinderland since I'd never seen that part before, and he was more than happy to show me around. He led me down a narrow path, past a large rain catchment tank, and over to a larger structure that had bunks built into the side. Perhaps it was because of the dim lighting, but I didn't even see a mist net above his sleeping area to keep out bugs, just a bunk and a huge tarp above it that covered all of the bunks in the area. Luckily, they were divided with walls.

He even had a few nooks for books, and he was happy to show me some. Sadly, I cannot recall any of the books that he had, but he was quick to say how happy he was at Cinderland. He told me that he used to live in the Midwest, but life here opened his heart up so much more than the mainland.

"Thanks for showing me this, Noah."

He flashed me a broad smile, his white teeth almost glowing in the night. "Of course, Andrew. I love showing where I live to my friends."

We wandered back over to the kitchen area, and I couldn't help but search for Selena's face among the crowd. Nothing.

I turned back around to the central table to see if they needed any more help, and I froze.

There she was, wearing a green shawl and talking to another resident of the community. Immediately, my heart felt like it was in my throat. I raised my hand and waved. "Hey!"

She turned, her eyes widening when she saw me. "Hey, how are you?"

"Great!" I said, feeling quite great indeed. "I really enjoyed talking with you the other day."

"Me, too!" Her eyebrows danced as she spoke.

"I wanted to ask you before I forget, do you want to exchange phone numbers and hang out some time?"

"Yes!" was her instant reply.

We exchanged numbers, and the rest of our conversation flew by in a blur. Then someone called out "Circle!" and we all circled around the space, singing the traditional circle song as we did every week.

After the song, I decided to stay cool and didn't look for her in the crowd of people dancing around the fire. Instead, I sat under the bunk beds, my usual spot, and enjoyed the drumbeat. Anansi sat nearby, and he started talking deeply, as he often did around me, about how the group dynamic felt to him that night. His insights were always interesting to me. He felt like a shaman or some kind of wizard, and only later did I learn that he was a massage therapist.

Still, I sensed something lingering in the back of his mind, some unspoken concern; and I made a mental note to keep an eye out for Lilith next time. I was curious why she didn't come to that incredible celebration of music and life. And then time seemed to wash away, and the night was filled with music, dancing, and joy.

CHAPTER 22

CAN I DRAW YOUR HANDS?

Not long after we'd exchanged phone numbers, I sent Selena a short text message, asking if she wanted to hang out at the tiny Pahoa library with me. Nestled up against the town's modest elementary school, I'd only been to the library once or twice before, and I felt that it would be a good, relaxing environment to get to know Selena better, a person who I increasingly couldn't get out of my mind.

The library was also air conditioned, which is a great bonus considering that August was one of the few months I ever felt uncomfortable with the weather on Hawaii. (The other was February, but we'll get to that.)

When I arrived, she was sitting on one of the low rock walls that framed the planters, wearing a dress streaked in the colors of the rainbow; and when she saw me, her eyes lit up, and she stretched out her arms for a hug. We embraced tightly and then headed over to the double doors.

Inside, we found a spot at one of the six rectangular tables, and I briefly excused myself to walk over to the oversized book section, thumbing through encyclopedias, directories, and histories until I found the object of my search: the big bird book.

I call it the big bird book because, for the life of me, I can't remember the title. Suffice to say that it was a huge book with beautiful illustrations of the birds of America, no doubt one of the many fine publications put out by the Audubon society.

When I returned to our table, I set the tome beside her, careful not to make too loud of a thud since there were people reading nearby.

"Check this out," I smiled. "A lot of incredible creatures in this one."

She smiled back, and together we thumbed through the large volume, admiring weird ducks, regal geese, and playful songbirds, stopping only occasionally so she could sketch one of the drawings for herself in her small notebook. Sometimes we would come across an especially silly looking bird, like a Sage Grouse or a Roseate Spoonbill, and stop for a moment, marveling at how strange it looked.

After a while, Selena pulled out a bigger sketchpad from her satchel and turned to me.

"Can I draw your hands?" she asked.

At first, I didn't know how to react. Even after plenty of dating adventures in Wisconsin, no one had ever asked me such a thing before.

"You want to draw my hands?" I said. "I mean, they're not *that* special."

"Yeah." She smiled. "You have nice hands."

"Thanks! So, how should I hold them? I mean, it's the first time someone has asked me that."

"It's okay. You don't have to do anything special."

"Okay."

I tried to distract myself while she drew. There are fewer things more aesthetically depressing than hands that look self-conscious, especially when they're the focus of a drawing, so I continued to peruse the bird book. After a while, I peeked over to her drawing pad, seeing a surprisingly lifelike rendering of one of my hands.

"Wow! That's really good!"

"You think so? It's a pretty quick sketch, but I like it."

Somehow, she had captured the essence of her subject. The hand in her drawing was undoubtedly mine, and I was touched.

From that day on, my mind was quite swept up in Selena's world, and we found any excuse to hang out. Some free time before Uncle Robert's? Let's go for a walk. Friday afternoon free? Let's do something.

I soon learned that she was helping out with one of the after school programs and loved working with children, which came as no surprise to me. And as the days washed by, she opened up to me more and more, telling me how an ex-boyfriend had left her earlier that year, for another woman, no less. But she assured me that the guy was no longer on the island.

Still, she seemed concerned about the situation. She didn't want ours to be a rebound relationship, and we agreed to take things slowly.

The following day, Hans, one of my newer friends from the Community, asked if I wanted to go on a little field trip with him to check out a piece of property he'd just bought on the east side of Puna, near the coast. I'd known Hans for a few weeks at that point, a middle aged guy who I found to be one of the most genuine people I'd met on the island yet.

So when he'd asked if I wanted to head up Government Beach Road, a route that ran along the eastern coast of the island, I didn't hesitate in saying yes. But on the way, we took a little detour down to the end of route 132, where it devolved into a dirt road, to Cape Kumukahi, the easternmost tip of the island.

Unlike South Point, there wasn't too much to do at the easternmost point. That might be why people don't even call it East Point. It was a rough piece of land, created by one of the countless lava flows that had formed the island over millennia. Most of it was sharp, jumbled lava rock, quite different from the undulating hills that I'd hiked over at the Kalapana lava fields.

There, the lava rock formed smooth wavy patterns, what the Hawaiians call pahoehoe (pah-hoy-hoy). East Point was the opposite, covered in fields of sharp, nearly impassable terrain the Hawaiians call ʻaʻā, which I can only imagine is from the sound one would make if one fell on it: Ah-AH!

So when we arrived, we didn't hike much, choosing to stay on the parts that had already been worn down a bit from foot traffic. Looking east, the waves crashed against long protrusions of lava rock that extended up from the ocean like long fingers, the water mixing and foaming all around them into beautiful blues.

To my right someone had made an elaborate memorial out of a pile of ʻaʻā, topped with a cross. In front of it was a cutout of what appeared to be the name MAKI, but there were so many shirts, leis, and other decorations that it was difficult to be sure.

I asked Hans about the memorial, and he guessed that someone must have died out here, perhaps on the rocks.

As we turned to head back to the car, I saw the Cape Kumukahi Light in the distance, a narrow steel-framed lighthouse that had been built in the 1930s and was somewhat famous for having survived the 1960 lava flow that destroyed the town of Kapoho. Yet when the flow reached the lighthouse, it split into two streams, spilling into the sea on either side.

Feeling satisfied, we took the Government Beach route northward, past the famously unmarked road that led to Cinderland and down a road that tunneled through thick rainforest. Through the thick foliage I could see that we were near the ocean at points, and after a while we made a second stop at an area with a slope that ran all the way down to the sea, covered in smooth boulders.

In a strange display, dozens of little towers made of round rocks had been stacked atop these boulders. And as the sun grew lower in the sky, the perfectly balanced towers, called cairns, appeared like eerie black silhouettes, their outlines almost human at times, standing like dark specters against the sapphire hues of the water below.

After photographing some of the more striking examples, we continued north, through the tunnel of green once more until we came to a housing development. Hans said that his plot of land was nearby, and before long I was standing on a decent little patch of dirt surrounded by trees, hints of other buildings peeking through the foliage.

His piece of land wasn't huge, but it was certainly big enough to build a house on and retire to, which is what Hans intended to do. He'd recently sealed the deal on the property, and his excitement was contagious. Listening to him talk about building a house here in paradise caused me to daydream about doing the same someday. After all, I didn't need that much space, and the land prices in Puna were some of the lowest in the state.

He took me down a narrow path that led through the forest to a backyard area, until we reached a stone wall. Beyond it, I could see a house in the distance. But overall, we were in an even more secluded area than before, and he said that he wanted to build a smaller structure out here. I smiled and agreed. It would be a beautiful spot for a tiny cabin.

I wondered what Selena would think of this place. Did she have a goal of getting a house on the island someday? I would have to ask her later. After all, we had dinner plans the following day, and the more I thought about it, the more excited I felt. It was going to be wonderful. Spending time with her always was.

On Friday, I met Selena at my favorite restaurant in downtown Pahoa, a delicious Thai establishment that was run by a family who actually were from Thailand. They'd brought their skills to Puna and soon formed a strong reputation through the sheer quality of their food.

We ordered pineapple curry, and somehow Selena's presence made it taste even better than when I'd first had it months earlier. Our conversation flowed effortlessly, and once again I felt shocked to have met someone that I clicked with so much. Back in Wisconsin, I'd gone on my fair share of dates, but too often the woman was on a totally different wavelength than mine or didn't have the qualities that I was looking for.

In comparison, Selena was like a breath of fresh air. And in the coming weeks, her playful energy and kindness felt like a soothing balm upon my heart, which was feeling increasingly burned by Matangi's attitude toward the Community.

Around this time, Matangi had accused me of misplacing a check. The only problem was, I had never been given any check. She berated me for not finding it, but after searching for it multiple times in all of the cabinets and desks, I finally gave up, telling her that I simply couldn't find it anywhere. She didn't seem to believe me, but I tried to be patient with her as I realized that it was quite likely that Matangi suffered from frequent bouts of acute anxiety. I tried to have empathy for her. After all, if I was trying to manage my business while travelling, I would probably be stressed, too.

During those times, Selena felt like a light of hope in an increasingly dark tunnel, and I struggled with what my next move would be. I didn't want to move into an even worse situation, and there were certainly some places that were a step down. Yet over time, they looked better and better.

I mentioned this to Selena during the dinner, asking if she knew of any communities that needed a web designer or a computer expert. She didn't know of any opportunities at the moment but was happy to keep a look out for me.

Not wanting to focus on the negative while spending time with one of the most wonderful people I'd met yet, I turned the conversation to the impending Perseid meteor shower. She said it had been years since she'd taken the time to see them, and she was excited to watch them together the following Monday, when the shower would reach its peak.

After dinner, we embraced tightly, and I felt the pull to kiss her. I remembered how she had been open with me about where she was emotionally, saying that she really liked me but wanted to take things slow since she was still healing from the breakup she'd mentioned earlier. So perhaps that's why, even given the perfect opportunity to kiss her that night, I didn't. The most she got was a kiss on the cheek.

As we hugged farewell, she squeezed my hand, and I saw a torrent of emotion swirling within her eyes. Would I be able to help her heal the wounds from her past? Would she even let me? Or was my presence only making things more confusing? All of these questions rolled around in my mind that night as I struggled to get comfortable in bed, simultaneously worried for the future and feeling elated about the present.

In the end, I focused on the fact that I couldn't predict the future. What was important was the present moment. At least we truly *did* care about each other. We had a strong heart-based connection, and I was so grateful for that.

CHAPTER 23

THE PERSEID SHOWER

On Monday, I couldn't wait to meet Selena at Island Naturals. She said that she wanted to make soup from some greens from her garden before they went bad but could meet me in town afterward, offering to bring some sprouts as a snack for later. I said that would be great and sautéed up a quick dinner before hitching up to Pahoa town, finding her sitting alone at one of the tables in front of the store, strumming a ukulele and singing to herself.

I called out to her, and she looked up, a smile filling her face. On the table, she had a glass juice jar and a few pages of songs, all of which were harvest themed, that she was practicing on her ukulele. She invited me to sing with her, and I happily did so.

As we sang, I couldn't help but find the combination of her voice and ukulele almost hypnotizing, and soon night had fallen.

After a while, we realized that we should get moving before it got too late and took her car southward to Isaac Hale Beach Park. We'd decided that it would be a fun place to see the meteor shower, and after we had parked, we walked around, looking for a suitable place to spread out her blanket and relax. The sky was mostly clear, and I took a moment to survey the thousands of stars over our heads.

The advantage of Isaac Hale Park was that it was easier to reach than Kehena Beach, not to mention less dangerous to walk to at night since the only way to get down to Kehena was a narrow, rather steep path. The only problem with Isaac Hale Park was that the nearby salt and pepper beach was mixed with sharp rocks, and we quickly realized that there was no way we were going to spread out the blanket there.

We turned our attention to a lifeguard tower, except that it wasn't really a tower. A small ramp led up to a little deck. Fabricated out of some plastic polymer, the lifeguard platform struck me as very strange until I realized that it was actually folded up. During the day, the front folded out and down, giving the lifeguard a clear view of the surf ahead.

The viewport was folded up, too, so we had plenty of room on the narrow deck, perhaps a meter wide, to spread out our blankets and relax. In moments, we realized that we had made the right decision. Whatever material this lifeguard platform was made out of, it was a lot more comfortable than the rocky beach below, and we leaned back and enjoyed the view of the galaxy spread out ahead of us in all of its majesty. At any moment, a bright meteor would streak across the sky; we just had to keep a sharp eye out.

We pulled out a couple snacks, and whenever one of us would turn our back to get something, the other would keep an eye out for any meteors.

"Look!" she shouted.

I whipped around, seeing nothing. "I guess I missed that one. They're pretty fast. Don't worry, we'll see more."

I leaned back down beside her, and as we held hands, I pointed out the W-shaped constellation called Cassiopeia which was slowly rising in the northeast sky ahead of us; and far above our heads, I noticed a frosty-bright star that I later confirmed was Vega, the fifth brightest star visible from Earth.

A bright streak crossed the sky, leaving a faint trail of crimson in its wake, a thin brushstroke of red across a black canvas, quickly fading.

"Whoa! Did you see that?"

"It's beautiful," she whispered.

As the night progressed, the meteor shower was forecasted to increase in density, and as we waited for more meteors, we talked about our favorite things: colors, foods, movies, and more. Somehow we got on the topic of the movie *Primer*, a low budget time-travel film that had a cult-like following.

"That reminds me of another movie," I said. "I think it's the same guy, too."

I struggled to recall the name of the movie.

"Oh," she said. "I think I know what you're talking about!"

"*Upstream Color!*" I said. "That's it; have you seen that?"

"Oh my gosh, yes! I loved that movie."

I blinked. "Wow, really? Every time I've mentioned that movie before, no one has even heard of it; but then again, it just came out this year. I can't believe you've seen it! It's a pretty strange story, isn't it? I mean, having the same creature go through all those different life cycles."

"Yeah, but I really enjoyed it. It's strange, but it's good. I can't believe you've seen it, too!"

"I love that one scene with them cuddling in the bathtub." I leaned over on my side to face her. "It reminds me of right here actually." I smiled, gazing into her hazel eyes.

Her gaze shifted to something far behind me. "Look!"

I turned around just in time to see a white flash, a meteor vaporizing in the blink of an eye as it burned up in the Earth's thick atmosphere.

"Beautiful."

We cuddled in the confined space of the lifeguard platform for a while longer, enjoying the meteors as they streaked above us. And as Cassiopeia rose higher and higher in the sky, we grew more sleepy. If we didn't move soon, we would fall asleep there, probably waking up to an annoyed lifeguard in the morning.

I turned to her. "Do you want to find a place to just spread out the blanket and sleep nearby?"

"Sure," she said. "I'm really sleepy, too."

We picked up our things and followed the sidewalk past the boat landing and down a narrow trail that led into the forest. A short while later, we came upon a spot that seemed secluded enough. No one would bother us there for a while, and we spread out.

I looked down to her smiling face, serene and happy; and for the first time, I kissed her gently. She kissed me back, and I kissed her again.

"Time for sleep," I whispered, pulling a blanket over us.

We got comfortable and fell asleep in minutes.

Several hours later, just as the tip of the constellation Orion was peeking over the horizon, it began to rain, lightly at first. Yet the rain grew in intensity until large drops splattered on my forehead, startling me awake. I looked up, seeing a sky utterly dark, stars blocked out by the thick clouds above.

"Hold on," I said, reflexively feeling my pocket to see if my iPod had gotten wet. It hadn't, and my hands raced to their next goal: my small daypack.

In a flash, I ruffled through the pack, finding my umbrella and expanding it over us as fast as I could. I checked my iPod; it was around 2:00 AM, and I tried to prop up the umbrella over us as we lay on the blanket, trying as hard as I could to avoid getting anything else wet. Then we huddled under the umbrella for some time until the rain finally passed.

Miraculously, sleep came over me once again, and I awoke several hours later to the first light of the morning. I rolled over as quietly as I could, checking to see how wet the contents of my daypack were. Only the top was slightly wet. The rain must have passed soon after we had fallen asleep. Relieved, I turned to Selena who was just beginning to open her eyes.

We stretched out, and she smiled at me. "You sleep okay?"

I laughed to myself, surveying our little spot in the faint dawn light for the first time. It was just a meter off of the trail.

Although my memory of this is slightly fuzzy, the rain started up again around that time.

I stood up and offered my hand down to her. She took it, and as I helped pull her to her feet, a smile spread across my face. "I think we should go for cover."

We quickly wrapped up our belongings and jogged back down to where the restroom structure was, across from the parking lot. The rain picked up, and we just looked at each other and laughed.

"How about we check out the warm ponds?" she said. "They're really pretty in the morning, and taking a quick swim would warm me up, too."

"Sounds fun!"

We waited a bit for the rain to let up before zipping over to her car, and I wondered if anyone had seen us during our unsanctioned sleepover. There were only a couple people around the boat landing area, so I didn't worry about it.

We took the short side-road down the coast, and when we arrived I was surprised to see that a huge pool had been constructed out of stone, complete with steps leading down to it. Selena said that the water was heated by a geothermal vent below, but as I would soon learn, there was a small opening at the east side that let in fresh, cool ocean water.

Officially known as Ahalanui County Beach Park, the warm ponds were a popular spot for locals to hang out. And as far as I can recall, that was the first time that I made it over there.

While I didn't know it at the time, I would swim in it wholeheartedly much later, sharing the water with Noah and some cool kids from another intentional community north of Pahoa. (I'm fairly sure they were all between the ages of 18 and 30, but I call them kids because of their bright, happy energy.)

But on that morning visit to the ponds with Selena, I didn't feel like swimming, instead preferring to stay dry and enjoy the vanilla morning light. Selena didn't mind and swam around nearby, telling me how much she loved the water. Thankfully, I'd brought a towel in my daypack, and it wasn't long before we were discussing breakfast as she dried herself off and brushed her long dark hair. Perhaps we ought to just get something quick at Island Naturals?

"Actually," she said, "they have fresh-baked pastries in the morning. They're really good! They have breakfast burritos, too."

It sounded great, so we drove up to Pahoa town. And as we walked into the store, I couldn't get the thought that we'd actually *slept over* at Isaac Hale Park out of my head, without anyone bothering us and without a tent. And as we surveyed the fresh goodies in the deli, I felt as if I was the keeper of some great secret.

Smiles filled our faces as we ate at one of the green tables in front of the store, and although we didn't talk much, it was a lovely breakfast. We didn't have to talk; we had shared something unforgettable. And across from us, I noticed a tiny dog sitting in a cloth shoulder-bag staring out onto passersby, totally content with where it was. I felt content, too.

CHAPTER 24

BREAKING THE STREAK

So I am going to state what I am sure you are never supposed to on a dating website: Based on your profile, I think I am in love with you.

Okay, so let's forget I ever uttered that craziness and continue with a more socially acceptable message.

Hi there. I came across your profile and I thought that you sounded like a truly incredible person. It sounds like you have been all over the place and that you have a lot of stories to tell, born from your imagination and from your life experiences both. I think I may envy you a little. But anyway, you sound like a really interesting person and I would love to get to know you.

(Obviously, I have no qualms about messaging first. Sadie Hawkins works for me! Although we never had one of those in high school, so I don't know if it would have actually worked for me...)

I hope to hear from you soon,
Dalasa

I received this message in the early hours on the following day, Tuesday the 13th; and when I finally read it that afternoon, I was at a loss for words.

For several years before Hawaii, I had used a dating website called OkCupid as a new way to meet interesting people who held values similar to my own. People use it to find romance, activity partners, friends, and everything in between.

To calculate compatibility, one answers a series of questions. The more questions one answers, the more accurate the matching system is. New users are prompted to answer the most popular questions first, and after about 50 questions or so, the system can find a good match within a specified radius of one's current location. Then one can read profiles of people with similar values, usually learning quite a bit from what people write as well as the photos they add to their profile. One only needs to send a good match a concise message and events roll on from there. Unsurprisingly, women receive far more messages than men.

When I lived in Wisconsin, I had used OkCupid to meet lots of interesting people, and over the course of a year or so, I learned a lot about myself and what I wanted in a relationship. (In fact, my hilarious adventures with online dating could probably fill a book on their own.)

The only problem was, if I was in an area without many OkCupid users, the system didn't work that well. And on the Big Island, that just wasn't how people preferred to meet. They more often met via a shared social circle or one of several hang out spots. For these reasons, I found that using the dating website was suboptimal on the Big Island. There were a couple interesting profiles, but overall the situation felt pretty limiting.

And honestly, I didn't feel much of a need to use the web to meet new people, anyway. During that time, I seldom even remembered that I *had* a dating profile. Through attending various markets and other weekly events, I had no shortage of opportunities to meet new people.

Still, OkCupid did have the potential to save me time, filtering through profiles to find those with especially similar values, without me having to meet everyone in Hilo. In short, I saw no reason to deactivate my profile, so I just let it sit there, passively attracting the occasional attention of people with values similar to mine.

Then Dalasa's message came in, and in the midst of all the ups and downs with Selena, I wasn't sure how to respond. In the end, I archived it for later. I just wasn't prepared to give the message the warm response it deserved.

On Tuesday morning, I asked Wayne if it was okay if Selena visited the Community that day. He said it would be fine. Actually, he was looking forward to meeting her, so that afternoon, I met her in town before leading her back to the Community. She enjoyed the playful nature of the place, and as we walked into the kitchen, I wished that the rules permitted me to let her stay the night for free.

It didn't surprise me that this had come up before with previous volunteers, but the rules were clear. She understood, and we made some food together before sitting down in the common area. I introduced her to Wayne and Anne-Marie, and soon we were all talking and laughing together.

At one point during dinner, Wayne pulled me aside and said that he and Anne-Marie liked Selena a lot. She was even more friendly and cool than they were expecting, and if I wanted, he said she could stay the night in my sleeping area for free.

"What do you mean?" I said, feeling slightly bewildered.

"What I'm saying is, I won't tell Matangi. This can be our secret." He sighed. "Dude, you work so hard. You've earned it."

I inhaled deeply, considering his offer.

"I don't know, man. That's really kind of you to think of me, but I don't wanna violate the rules here." Matangi's screaming face flashed into my mind, but I pushed it away. "Plus, it could get back to her. Some other volunteer could say something."

"Dude, no one's gonna say anything. They see how well you two go together. I honestly wouldn't worry about it."

I ran the idea by my gut, but still had mixed feelings. "Well," I paused, "I'll think about it."

Wayne nodded. "Your call."

After dinner, I showed her around the rest of the property, and we ended up near my sleeping quarters where we cuddled for a while. We listened to Vampire Weekend as it squeaked out of my tiny iPod speaker, and I sang softly. As we lay on our sides, I kissed her and gazed into the ocean of feeling behind her eyes.

"Wayne told me you could stay for free tonight if you wanted. I guess they really like you."

A mixture of expressions passed over her face. "Are you sure? I don't want to get you in trouble."

"I'm sure."

Selena winced, pressing her eyes shut as if she were suddenly in pain. "Oh, but I shouldn't." Her eyes flashed open. "I don't know. To be honest, staying the night feels too fast for me. Andrew, I'm worried that I'm *using* you."

I felt my expression twist in stunned confusion. "What do you mean? I thought you said you were over him."

"Well, I think I am, but what if I'm really not?" Her expression softened. "I just don't want to hurt you, Andrew."

"I understand." I paused to reflect on her words. "Here's the thing: you won't hurt me. You've told me your situation. I'm well aware of it, so the chances of anyone getting hurt are a lot lower. Anyway, we can go as slowly as you want." I paused, inhaling deeply. "Selena, I don't have expectations of you. I just like spending time with you."

Behind her eyes, a heady mixture of sadness, hesitation, and hopefulness swirled together. "Okay," she finally said, "no expectations. But I can't stay tonight."

"That's okay."

We snuggled for a while longer until we realized it was almost midnight, and as I kissed her goodbye, tension tugged at my heart. As I waved goodbye to her, an uneasiness came over me, and I wondered if I'd been too affectionate somehow.

The following week went by in a blur. I managed to get some writing time in on Thursday and Friday, feeling good about refocusing on my work and enjoying some breathing room after what had been a whirlwind of a week for both of us.

On my weekend shift, Matangi further increased her expectations of me as the slow weeks of the summer were coming to an end. And all three of us long-term volunteers were working harder than ever before.

Thankfully, one of the volunteers, Jane, wanted to become the fourth long-term volunteer and turned out to be fantastic at communicating with everyone at the Community.

Jane's presence made the work of running the Community a bit lighter for everyone, but less so for me since Matangi seemed to expect even more web design and computer-related work once Jane started. On the face of it, this would have been reasonable, if she hadn't already assigned me more than enough work to fill all of my hours.

Still, she wasn't the first person I'd worked with that didn't understand how long it would take to implement a new feature, not to mention the complexity of doing some of the things she wanted done. She just wanted them done and expressed little concern in understanding why certain things took longer than others. By this time, it was obvious to me that she had relied on a string of computer-savvy volunteers since the place had begun, but had only learned the basics for herself. This attitude in and of itself is understandable. As a business owner, she had a lot on her plate. The only problem was, no matter how much I did for her,

198 · BREAKING THE STREAK

she didn't seem to trust me. And her expectations never came down to Earth.

Early the following week, I texted Selena that I'd like to see her, but she seemed pretty busy. In the end, she said that she had a short time to talk if I could meet her at the library, which was near the school.

When I arrived, she was wearing the rainbow dress that had brought a smile to my face the week before, and we embraced tightly. She told me she didn't have much time but that she really enjoyed visiting the Community and meeting my friends. She said a friend from the mainland was coming to visit her soon. This change would make her life more busy, but she wanted her friend to meet me when they had some free time.

After a short while, she said she had to go. We hugged again, and I wished her a great day with the after school program. She flashed me a big smile and sprinted away, disappearing behind a yellow building.

For a full week, I didn't see even a glimpse of her.

I wasn't entirely surprised. Clearly, she was still processing a lot from her previous relationship, and I didn't lose all hope. She would text me from time to time, saying that she was thinking of me or to wish me a good work shift at the Community. Later in the week, she even invited me to a party the following Friday.

The invite buoyed my confidence, but I couldn't help but feel that she was pulling away. As much as I didn't want to believe it, the thought that perhaps she just wasn't *ready* for a new relationship began to gnaw at the back of my mind.

To be frank, writing these experiences down was actually quite difficult at points because it made plain some early warning signs that would become problems later. It also stung to realize that, by this point, I usually had to initiate the dialogue if I wanted to see her at all, a classic sign of pulling away.

On Monday, I did just that, saying that I wanted to say hello, even if it was just for a few minutes. She responded, saying that she was too busy that morning but that she could meet after work; so later that day I hitchhiked into town to get some groceries before meeting her at the library once again. As usual, seeing her brought a big smile to my face, and this time, she'd brought her friend with her.

My first impression of Zusa was that she was sassy, fun, and seemed much older than Selena in the way that she carried herself, even though they were about the same age. It turned out that they had more free time than they had anticipated, and Selena offered to give me a ride back to the Community.

I gratefully accepted, and since it was still light out when we arrived, I asked them if they wanted a brief tour of the property. They both were enthusiastic about the idea, and I led them around the more interesting parts of the property, which, in the interest of anonymity, I will refrain from describing. Suffice to say, we had fun exploring the rainforest.

Afterward, all three of us prepared some delicious vegetarian food in the kitchen. And when Wayne and Anne-Marie showed up, the gathering transformed itself into a dance party. Selena and I held hands as we danced, smiling at each other like fools, and I felt my heart singing.

Still, a feeling of uneasiness was mixed in, too; and I remembered what she'd said. I shouldn't get attached, I told myself. I have no idea how this woman is going to feel about our connection tomorrow.

The rest of the night went by in a blur, and I didn't even bother asking Selena if she wanted to stay over. Curiously enough, Wayne and Anne-Marie later told me that they thought Zusa was pretty eccentric, but they still liked Selena.

I tried to see it from their perspective. Zusa had seemed mildly neurotic in a way that was difficult to pin down, but it hadn't been as noticeable to me as it apparently was to them. What *else* was I missing?

Later in the week, Selena texted me, saying that she wanted to have a phone call about the party that she'd invited me to on Friday. Unfortunately, my cheap cell phone had recently gotten slightly wet and was spending some quality time in a bag of rice to dry out. With my phone out of commission, I could only text via my iPod. Still, perhaps it was for the best, I thought. It would be better if we met up in person to talk, anyway.

The following day was Friday, and I texted her back, asking if she had some time to talk before work, but once again she seemed unable to make even a five minute gap in her morning to speak with me. And several hours later, my iPod practically exploded with the length of texts that came in, explaining that she didn't think it would be a good idea for me to come to the party that evening, after all.

To my horror, she said that her ex-boyfriend was back on the island. Even worse, he had been invited to the same party. She explained how she felt very guilty about it, but she had to disinvite me from the party. She felt like it was all too much if we were both there and apologized, saying that she needed to go slowly and felt that it hadn't been slow for her.

At reading all of this, I fell back onto my chair, stunned. My first thoughts were ones of anger and betrayal. How could she disinvite me to a party the *same day* it was happening? Part of me understood where she was coming from, but the way that she sprang it on me at the last minute made me feel disrespected. No wonder she'd wanted to speak over the phone, but after I told her that my phone was broken, she didn't seem to make an effort to speak to me any other way.

Perhaps it was my fault. Perhaps I should have borrowed someone's phone, but in her texts she hadn't made it sound urgent. If she had, I would have borrowed Wayne or Anne's phone without hesitation; they would have been happy to help. Looking back on it, this situation was yet another example of how meaning and tone can be lost when sending text messages. I have since learned to be much more careful, and experience has given me a certain amount of intuition around what people really mean when they text me.

As the feeling of shock wore off, it simmered down into a salty pot of sadness mixed with shame, like the emotion itself had been sitting on the stove for too long and became a saucy reduction that was too bitter to stomach. At first, I was at a loss at how to respond to her rejection, and ended up showing the single, longwinded text message to Clarence, a middle-aged man who had recently left the tech sector to start his own farm on the island. He had moved into the sleeping area nearest to me, effectively becoming my roommate. Thankfully, he had a lot of life experience and was honest and compassionate toward me.

I shook my head as he read the message on my iPod, reiterating that I honestly didn't know where to go from there, at least, not at that moment. And my gaze burned into the ferns beyond the small window of our quarters.

He looked up from the screen, his expression stiffening. "I'm sorry, Andrew. It sounds like she feels overwhelmed."

My eyes remained fixed on the greenery outside. "Yeah."

"Well, all you can do at this point is give her space. Tell her you understand and give her time."

I nodded slightly, mulling over his words before turning to him. "Thanks for looking at it. Yeah, I think you're right."

In my heart, all the events of the week, the distance, the missed connections—all of it swirled together inside of me, making me numb. I'd been so excited about seeing her again, not to mention meeting more new people at the party.

Still, hearing Clarence's words gave me a small sense of peace in that mixed up time, and I vowed to find some positive perspective on the situation.

After all, it was still Friday morning. The whole day was open to me, and without any concrete plan, I hitchhiked up to Pahoa to do something that almost always cheered me up: I went to wander. Even in a town as comparatively small as Pahoa, there are hundreds of little nooks and hidden places within walking distance that most people who visit will never see.

I wandered down streets and found where they ended, giving way to thick forest and strange trails. In the end though, my hunger got the best of me, and I went back to Main Street to get some food, discovering that the small fruit stand I'd visited many times before was gone. What had happened? I walked farther down the sidewalk, and to my relief, the same shop had grown into a new location. Far more spacious than the previous food stand setup, the business had moved into an actual commercial space. It was small, but it was a real store.

I walked in and saw Dez behind the counter at the far end of the room. To either side, dozens of varieties of exotic, brilliantly colorful fruits were on display on slanted wooden tables. Relaxing music oozed from a speaker atop a large white refrigerator; and upon seeing me, Dez smiled, waving me inside.

CHAPTER 25

TRANSFERENCE & PAIN

"Hey, there!" Dez called out, "How ya doin'?"

I smiled back to her. "Lot going on right now. Is this your new location?" I walked up and sat down at the stool in front of the counter. Ahead, Dez sat behind a black computer monitor, a small donation bin, and a carefully arranged collection of star fruit in a basket.

"It's a big step up!" I said. "I really like it."

"Thanks! It was a real challenge, but we did the whole move in about two days. We're really proud of the new place."

As usual, Dez made me feel right at home. We "talked story" for a while (a local term which basically means sharing news and stories). And when customers would eventually make their way down to the end of the store where the checkout was, we would invariably have interesting, and often hilarious, conversations about what was going on. To say that the customers came in a colorful variety may be an understatement, and after a while, Dez and I joked that we should put a microphone somewhere and record some of the funny conversations and turn them into comic strips or stories later.

After a while, Dez asked me if I could do her a favor and grab her and her boyfriend a couple chicken Caesar salads at the Cash & Carry store down the street.

"Sure!" I said. "I'd be happy to."

"Oh, and can you grab a bag of Maui onion chips, too? Here's my card."

By that time, I had visited Dez and her boyfriend's fruit stand many times, and we had built up a healthy level of trust. So her request didn't really surprise me.

"I'll be right back." I said, taking her credit card and heading down the street.

"Thanks, Andrew!" she called back, the sound of a smile in her voice.

Perhaps it was because homeless people were almost always loitering out in front, but as I approached the somewhat generic white building, I realized that I'd never actually been inside the Cash & Carry before. I crossed the street and walked in, quickly realizing that the interior was a bizarre maze of perpendicular aisles, and the floor itself was a hodgepodge of dirty white tile. Clearly, this place had been expanded several times, but in the cheapest way possible. Still, it's not like there was that much money flowing through Pahoa at the time. I'm sure they were doing the best that they could.

I navigated the rather confusing store and found the Caesar salads and the chips. At seeing the chicken in the salads, I couldn't help but wince. A living creature with a brain had to die to make that meal possible, and back then, even before I'd learned more about the meat industry, I felt conflict in seeing those products.

When I got back to the store a few minutes later, Dez smiled in gratitude.

"Thank you so much, Andrew! That really saved me time."

"Of course."

We talked story for a bit longer.

I mentioned my challenges with Selena, and Dez listened carefully. In the end, she recommended that I give Selena more time and space, and I agreed.

By then, the afternoon had worn on, and I told Dez that I should be getting back. I didn't want to get stuck hitchhiking at night if I could help it. She bid me a warm farewell, and soon I was in a car heading back to the Community.

Later that day, I talked to Wayne again, and he told me something that was so encouraging that I had to write it down after we talked.

It had been a while since we'd sat down and caught up. He told me about how he didn't see his father much when he was growing up because he was in the military, and I silently felt thankful that, while my father *did* work a lot, I still saw him almost every day when I was a kid.

Wayne and Anne-Marie had lived all over the country, trying out different places. Anne-Marie had been the one who had found the Community's website and the managing opportunity, and after some convincing on her part, he agreed that they would come to the Big Island and check it out. They'd arrived about three weeks before I had, and I asked him if Matangi had seemed critical of them when they'd arrived.

"Not really," Wayne said, "but remember how I told you that they called you the 'Male Molly' before you got here? You and Molly had a lot of concerns in common. She was a tech person, too. I heard Molly had a lot of problems integrating here, and I think a lot of transference happened when you arrived. Matangi expected you to be like Molly and looked for information to confirm her stereotype of you."

I shook my head. "That's terrible."

"She stereotyped me, too. In her eyes, I'm the builder and landscaping guy. Matangi puts people in boxes, Andrew, and it's not fair to any of us. And you have been so consistent in your work. I see it, and Anne-Marie does, too."

"Thanks." I smiled. "Even so, Matangi doesn't seem to have any tolerance for mistakes. I made one mistake about what to photograph. Once! And then she calls into question all of my experience in photography and Photoshop. I've been doing that stuff for over 10 years, and she thinks I'm useless in that area now because of that one mistake." I looked up, peering into his dark eyes.

"Andrew," he said, growing more serious, "you are obviously challenging to her, and she's tired of it. So just be supportive. Play her game to *your* end."

"What do you mean?"

"I mean, if you feel used, then turn it around. Finish your book. Use this place like it uses you."

I considered his words. "Yeah... Well, I *am* going to finish it. I guess it's just hard because, except for you and Anne-Marie, every person I've clicked with here at the Community has left. Even Greg left. And now Selena is acting like she doesn't even want to see me. It's hard to write in the midst of all that. It just makes me sad, Wayne, and I'm starting to feel like I don't even belong here anymore."

Concern spread over Wayne's face. "Stay true to yourself. You speak positive catalyst into people's lives, Andrew." His eyes burned with conviction. "Remember that."

That weekend was the calm before the storm.

Writing about this part of 2013 was the most difficult part of this book to relate because of the toxicity and vitriol that was dished out to me. Combined with Selena's push-pull attitude toward our relationship, it all culminated into a week that I will never forget. And to retell the story of that tumultuous week as accurately as possible, I have carefully reviewed all of the emails Matangi and I exchanged that month.

At first, it started innocuously: a few changes with the layout of one of the web pages. Matangi had some of the information on the site organized with tables, and that weekend it was my job to log into the content management system and update some of those tables with new information.

I had been working with this system, called Wordpress, for over five years at that point, but I hadn't used tables for layout in a while since none of my client work had lent itself to displaying information that way. Without getting too technical, these tables were made using some special code so that we could align the images inside them correctly.

To be clear, I didn't mind using tables in some of the Community website pages. The only problem was that Wordpress sometimes removed the formatting code within the tables when I updated the page. Tables are an older way to organize information, and each time I saved the page, I had to check and see what the published webpage looked like to make sure that the system didn't remove any code. If it did, the tables would arrange the photos in a weird way, so when I finished up my work on Sunday, I made sure to check that the published webpages looked good. And they did.

Then, after my work shift ended later that evening, I decided to stop worrying about the website and finally respond to Dalasa's message. She had waited for five days, after all.

Wow, that's really sweet! I'm not sure when I'll be in Hilo next, but perhaps we can meet up next time :)

In retrospect, I wish I would have written more. After all, she had written such a warm, friendly message. But there was just too much going on for me to know when I would be back in Hilo, which was where she lived. If things were meant to work out, then I would meet her, but for now, I had to take it one day at a time.

The camel's back broke the next day.

When I checked my email on Monday morning, I noticed that I had received a message just after midnight. It was a short message from Matangi, written in all capital letters, demanding that I check the volunteer to-do list immediately. I knew that Matangi intended to shout in the email because she ended the email in all capital letters saying that she was, in fact, shouting and used a four-letter word that no boss had hurled at me before, or since.

What the heck? What had I done to deserve that?

I checked the to-do list and saw a series of messages that had been posted late into the night. It started out rather calmly, asking why the formatting was different. Then it grew into all caps, asking me to fix it as soon as possible. The next comment was even angrier, saying that another page had the same formatting problem. Matangi said that I was testing her patience and asked me if I'd deliberately screwed up the website for fun.

I felt stunned. I had checked the pages the night before, and they'd looked fine. Unless another volunteer had gone in and edited a page late into the night, an unlikely scenario, there shouldn't have been a problem.

As I read her messages, I felt more and more depressed and disrespected, and I wrote a multi-paragraph message in response. I felt hurt that, after all of the quality work that I'd done for her, she thought I would jumble the website's layout for fun. In my message, I made it clear to her that I would never sabotage my own work and reiterated that I was proud of the graphic design, photography, and coding work that I'd done since I'd been there.

And when she swore at me, it made me question if she valued my work at all. No one in a managerial position over me had ever slung such vitriol at me before, and I defended myself concisely, saying that the page did not look that way when I'd checked it the previous night.

I fixed the two web pages that were jumbled and showed Wayne and Anne-Marie my message to Matangi. They read the whole message thread and said that they felt very sorry, and even ashamed, for how Matangi was treating me. They helped me reword a couple paragraphs in my response to her, and as I sent off the message, I felt numb. Even though Matangi and I had miscommunications sometimes, I still respected her for what she'd built at the Community. To read her messages crushed me, and I knew that things would never be the same after that day.

I even talked about it with my father, who is good at dealing with challenging circumstances. Even more importantly, he always had my back. My father said that he thought I'd handled it as best as I could and told me to hang in there.

At that low time, his encouragement meant a great deal.

The following day, I received a response from Dalasa.

Lol, well I do appreciate that I'm sweet, rather than certifiable :) I would very much like to get together next time you're in Hilo. Just let me know when and we can see if we can work something out!

Her response brightened my mood. Her patience felt refreshing, and I made a mental note to message her again once things calmed down.

I also received a long email from Matangi, apologizing for swearing and accusing me of sabotaging my work. That was a good sign, but she also made it clear that she *wasn't* apologizing for being angry, saying that it was the straw that broke the camel's back.

She went on to say that she had already cancelled any landscaping or photo work for me because of delays, difficulties, or what she had perceived as inability.

Her words cut into my heart like tiny knives. I felt like reminding her that she had brought me on specifically as a technology consultant and web specialist, not as a landscaper, but I came to realize that it wasn't worth it.

I no longer wanted to be there.

In the final section of her email, she said that she *had* opened the page with the tables. She asked if the act of opening it in the editing mode could change the code, and I realized that she must have saved the web page after making an edit. Was it possible that Matangi had broken the page herself and not even realized it? Had she not realized that the page had looked great *before* she'd edited it, or had she gone directly to edit it and never even looked at the published webpage first?

With that statement, she admitted that she had caused the problem that she had slung so much negativity toward me for. But would she be able to understand that was possible? After all, she wasn't technically-minded.

Matangi closed the email by saying that she was probably running out of web design work for me. But the cherry on top was toward the end of her message: she asked if I had any diagnosed behavioral conditions that I hadn't told her about.

No employer, not to mention any client, had ever questioned my mental condition before.

I found it challenging to avoid feeling insulted. I told Wayne and Anne-Marie about her response, and once again they were shocked. I wasn't sure how to respond; I still felt numb from the whole experience, and Wayne assured me that we would deal with the situation together.

Going forward, we decided to be as positive as possible with Matangi; and I responded as politely as I could, saying that none of my bosses, teachers, or family had ever raised concerns about any behavioral conditions whatsoever. I finished my message on a positive note, reinforcing that Wayne, Anne-Marie, and I had talked about some new projects for me and that it was important to me to keep moving forward in a positive direction.

Matangi responded about two hours later by giving me a written warning. Without getting into too much detail, the Community had recently received a negative review on the internet from two previous guests, and I had been the volunteer on duty when they were staying. They had mentioned something about a cockroach, a common visitor on island properties, in their sleeping space and had complained about the kitchen area being dirty.

Matangi also brought up the lost check that Greg had said he'd left with me, even though I'd never touched it.

As I read the email, I felt as if each of her words was like a small pebble that I was being forced to swallow. Soon, my stomach would fill up, and I would explode. That was the first I'd heard about a negative review. Such a review could hurt the public perception of the Community, and I felt terrible.

I retraced my memory and talked to Wayne, discovering that the complaining guests must have stayed the night when the Community had a small party. I had put in a lot of website work that day, and my brain had felt fuzzy. I was so tired that I'd even gone to bed only an hour after my shift ended. And when I woke up the following morning, the kitchen had been a mess.

That was bound to happen in a shared space, and I didn't give it a second thought. I had checked the guest's sleeping area before they'd checked in, and it had been clean.

In my response to Matangi, I reassured her that I did prepare their sleeping area ahead of time and that it was in great condition. Wayne, Anne, and I talked about that night, and we agreed that we'd never seen a cockroach or even a frog in that particular space. Still, I was responsible for their experience while I was on duty, and I apologized, wondering if perhaps being distracted by Selena was adversely affecting my performance.

But what was I supposed to do? I had done my job, and Wayne suspected that the couple simply weren't ready for the unique, and somewhat disorganized, environment of the Community. And it wasn't our job to make sure the kitchen was clean all of the time, either, only during our work shifts.

I reflected on how to proceed. As much as I'd tried to put my best foot forward, as hard and consistently as I'd worked for Matangi, I came to accept the fact that we just didn't work well together. I should have accepted it sooner, but at the time, I didn't want to believe it. After all, her Community attracted such smart and interesting people, but things had come to a head.

That week, I finally made peace with the fact that, even though I cared about Wayne and Anne-Marie very much, I *had* to leave the Community as soon as I could and find a decent alternative, one that didn't feel toxic.

I sent my Dad a little update on the situation and asked that he intend for a positive outcome, that I would find another place that needed my computer skills. He said that he and Mom would be praying for me, and that meant a lot.

Several weeks later, I heard that Wayne came across the missing check under a random pile of junk. I had not put it there, because I had never been given it. Perhaps Greg had misplaced it before he'd left and forgot.

Honestly, we would never know, and after all of her anger about the check, Matangi offered no apology to anyone.

CHAPTER 26

ASKING THE UNIVERSE

In retrospect, it was truly remarkable how quickly so many opportunities came to me once I fully accepted that I was leaving the Community.

It was almost as if I'd set off a domino effect just by changing my attitude. The sheer amount of new people and experiences that came into my life in September is stunning to me in retrospect. And looking back, I can't say I'm entirely surprised. Time and again, my life has shown me that once I am in alignment with what I want, events and people are allowed to flow freely, and the dominos fall with remarkable speed.

The first of these dominos was Molly, the volunteer who had come to the island with concerns similar to mine, coming back into the picture. She'd stayed on the island, but rarely visited the Community. In retrospect, our situations had been similar, except that she hadn't tolerated Matangi for as long.

Why *had* I tolerated her critical attitude for so long?

Now with the benefit of over three years of reflection since that final month, I must admit that it was primarily due to fear and perhaps even a bit of laziness. I was afraid that I wouldn't find another place where I could do work that I enjoyed. Every other community I found seemed to only need people to pull weeds or dig holes. To be clear, I have no problem with that type of work. I have tremendous respect for people who work the land, but I preferred to do the technical work that I had spent years becoming highly skilled in.

On top of that, I actually started to *believe* the things that Matangi would hint at in conversations, that the Community was the best place on the island, that everywhere else was either overpriced or probably full of dangerous people.

Of course, where I lived was entirely my responsibility, and finding another place would take a lot of work. In retrospect, I could have found a place sooner, but I was holding out for a great match. But would that pay off? Plus, I would really miss Wayne and Anne-Marie.

By the time August rolled around, Molly was occasionally stopping by the Community to say hello to us. She had since moved on to a different work-trade opportunity, but I soon realized that we were nonetheless in a similar situation. We were both dissatisfied with where we currently were and wanted to make a change. After talking for a while, she mentioned that she would be driving over to a bigger community nearby and asked me if I wanted to come.

"Sure!" was my near-instant reply.

A couple days later, I found myself in her car, heading down one of the two lane highways that cut through the island. From the highway, it was really easy to see how the entire island really was one massive mountain, and in the distance, I could see the Pacific Ocean far below, glistening in the morning light.

When we arrived, I was shocked at the sheer size of the larger community. It had much better facilities and much more land than where I had been staying. This community was more self-contained, too; and I considered the risk that staying there might distract me from exploring the island more. What if all of the social events clouded my primary goal which was to explore?

In the days before, I had studied their website to see where I might fit in best. I tried to speak to the person who was in charge of web design, but to my disappointment he was on vacation.

Even so, I was happy to talk with one of the other tech guys, and he seemed positive that I had a good shot for being a work-trade volunteer there, perhaps even working up to a paid position. He gave me the email of the guy who led their website development and went on his way. Something about the way he zipped away stuck in my mind for a while. There was something almost foreign about it. What was it?

Of course. The interaction didn't have the warmth of nearly every other conversation I'd had on the island. It was more hurried, more hustle-and-bustle. We rounded out our tour by walking past some newly built tiny houses in a field in the distance. Molly thought that they were only for permanent residents. They were certainly the highest quality living structures I'd seen on that property.

When we got back to the Community, I wrote an email to the lead tech guy, pitching him on my wide array of skills and depth of knowledge from Wordpress to Photoshop and beyond. I hoped that it wouldn't take too long to hear back from him.

Around this time, I received a short text message from Selena, asking me if I wanted to join her at the community I'd just visited for a spirit collage class on Sunday. I didn't know what a spirit collage was, but I would have gone to an electric flea circus if she'd asked. Thankfully, Wayne was happy to swap work shifts with me, saying that he was excited that I would get to see Selena after such a challenging week.

I texted her back, saying that I would be happy to join her, and after a relatively uneventful work shift when I paid special attention to respond to Matangi's messages even faster than before, I breathed a sigh of relief and looked forward to seeing Selena again.

Sunday was a good day.

Selena had given me a rough idea of where the class was going to be, and I found the outdoor classroom area without much trouble. Plenty of paint, magazines, and various other fiddly bits of paper had been left out where a half dozen people were eagerly awaiting instructions. I walked up to the group, and when Selena turned around, a big smile spread across her face.

"I'm so glad you could make it!" she beamed, but her expression melted into concern. "I hope it wasn't too inconvenient coming here on a Sunday. I heard about it, and I thought it would be a fun thing for us to do. I'm so glad you could make it!"

I shook my head. "No, it wasn't too much trouble. We volunteers swap work shifts sometimes. It's not a big deal."

The instructor explained that the first step was to go through the stack of magazines, tear out any images that inspired us, and save them. She said that we'd begun late, so we'd have to go fast to have enough time.

And so, we sat down around a long table and made funny rustling sounds with the magazines as we rummaged through them, zipping through hundreds of photos. Within the piles, the selection ranged from food magazines to editions of National Geographic. Images of stunning architecture, computers, and food caught my eye, and I tore out and saved some photos that resonated with me. After perhaps 15 minutes, the instructor told us to stop and let us all cut out a large section of poster board, encouraging us to cut it into any shape we wanted.

Feeling like I could use a hexagon in my life, I cut out a wide hexagon, so that the sides were flat and the top and bottom came to a gradual point. I'd certainly never seen a collage that shape before, and I was happy with it.

All of us used glue sticks to affix our images to the poster board, sometimes cutting the photo into an interesting shape before gluing it and sometimes leaving a ragged edge for the sheer heck of it.

In the end, my collage was a strange combination of stunning architecture surrounded by water, some computers, and food. It wasn't exactly what I was going for.

Selena's was more focused on dancing and expression, and I liked hers more.

The outdoor class ended, and as we rolled up our spirit collages, I wondered if what my spirit *really* wanted that day was some delicious food. I didn't feel especially hungry, but it was pretty ridiculous how much food was in my collage.

As Selena and I walked back to the road, I thanked her for inviting me, and I got the distinct feeling that she was still in conflict about our relationship. Part of her was afraid, and part of her wanted to embrace the new possibility. I could feel it.

Somehow, we got to talking about intention-manifestation. Also known as the Law of Attraction, the idea is that one can bring what one wants into their life by consistent visualization and clarity. By doing this, one is more likely to take the actions that bring one's desires into reality. In recent years, some teachers have popularized this idea in movies and books, but unfortunately they have focused primarily on bringing in material possessions to the exclusion of all else.

In my experience though, manifestation can happen much faster if one isn't asking for something material. Asking the Universe for an *opportunity* has been more effective for me than asking for money, for instance, especially if it isn't just for my own gain. When I am in complete alignment with an intention, when every part of me agrees, things manifest the fastest. Even money. And intentions that align with an attitude of service and generosity tend to flow into my life much more effortlessly.

When we reached the road, I told Selena that I bet I could manifest a ride in under a minute. She squinted at me, incredulous. After all, it was pretty late, and traffic tended to grow thinner as dusk approached.

I only smiled back to her and stuck out my thumb. I had an unusually good feeling about manifesting a ride quickly, and to my delight, a car pulled over to the side of the road just 15 seconds later. Selena looked over to me, a mixture of shock and elation filling her face.

Perhaps it was only luck. All I can say for sure was that I rarely got such a feeling of certainty out of nowhere, and on those rare times, I almost always acted on it because that's when I saw magic truly happen.

Often, the best things that happen to me are improbable, and the improbability continued well after we were already cruising down the road. The driver said that, before she got back into town, she wanted to stop and wish happy birthday to someone living out on the lava and hoped we didn't mind. Apparently there was a little party out on the lava, and she asked if we'd like to join her. We agreed without hesitation. After all, parties out on the Kalapana lava field are special. On the drive over, the sun slipped below the horizon, and the stars shone over us like tiny jewels, so clear that I almost felt like I could touch them.

When we arrived, we were swept up in a strange swirl of music, fluffy cake, and happy people. As I wandered around the second floor of a house that was still partially under construction, I walked out onto the deck, stunned that a full, five person band was set up under bright lights. Three guitars, a keyboardist, and a drummer were radiating happy tunes.

Whoever's birthday it was, they had no shortage of friends, and Selena and I danced for a while, feeling so grateful that we'd been spontaneously invited to the party. Selena danced with a piece of cake in her hand, yellow sari wrapped around her body, and I snapped a photo so that I would never forget that moment. Seeing her having fun filled me with so much happiness.

We stayed for perhaps an hour and a half before our ride took us back up to the familiar four way intersection just south of Pahoa. We hugged and went our separate ways. And as I caught a ride going in my direction, my head was still spinning from our unforgettable day. With a rolled up spirit collage in my hand, I rode into the dark jungle, reflecting in gratitude for my life on that remarkable island.

CHAPTER 27

TARA THE MEDITATOR

On the day I met Tara, I was hitchhiking back to the Community after some coastal explorations, and as I held my thumb outstretched, she pulled her car over to the grassy shoulder of the road, waving me in.

Her sharp smile and positive attitude made me feel at ease, and soon we were cruising down the road, chatting along as if we'd known each other for years. She asked me what brought me to the island, and I said something like, "Adventure."

I told her that I was writing my second book, a science fiction adventure with a tropical twist, and she was intrigued. She asked me where I was staying, and I told her about the Community and how I was on the lookout for a better place.

Even though we'd just met, something inside me told me that I could trust her implicitly. As we continued talking, she asked me more about my situation, and I realized that I felt comfortable sharing with her how Matangi had treated me during my stay. Tara listened carefully, expressing concern and disappointment at how I was being mistreated, and I asked her if she knew of any other communities looking for a web specialist.

To my surprise, she said she lived in a guest house near a meditation center, and she'd been looking for someone like me.

"Why me?" I asked.

We reached the Community entrance, and Tara pulled over to the side of the road and turned to me, a new energy filling her voice. For years, she had been working on a book that she saw as the first step in her life's work. Into the book, she had poured just about every good idea she'd come across from her research into conservation, meditation, and philosophy. The process had taken years and had left her with a manuscript spanning over 150,000 words, over 500 pages.

The only problem was, nearly everyone she had shown it to said that it had some serious pacing problems, not to mention some plot points that stretched scientific believability, even for a book in the thriller genre. After all, it was her first book, and one's first book seldom turns out quite how they want it to.

She had worked hard to rewrite parts of the story, but as her patience wore, her back pain grew worse, and she decided to take some time off, turning her focus to healing her body. In the process, she tried dozens of techniques to treat her chronic pain.

All the while, she considered the idea of working with someone, a professional content editor or writer to restructure the book to be the fast-paced thriller that she always wanted it to be, which is where I came in.

Tara put the car in park. She asked me lots of detailed questions about how I'd published my books, what reviews my first book had gotten, and where she could look me up.

I was happy to share all of this with her. I had published independently to have the most control over my content, as well as my price. At that point, my first book, *The Truth Beyond the Sky*, had only been out for about nine months, and it had gotten dozens glowing reviews on Amazon alone. In fact, many of the reviews were multiple paragraphs long.

The more I told her, the more she seemed to smile. She said that we would have to meet again soon and go over some details, but work-trading with her seemed like a good proposition. Furthermore, there was a 10-day silent meditation retreat coming up in two weeks, and she highly recommended that I attend if I was serious about work-trading with her and helping with the book.

It all seemed familiar somehow.

"Wait a minute," I said. "Months ago, I met a woman named Sandi who was raving about that retreat. Is she still there?"

"Really? You met Sandi? Perhaps we were *supposed* to meet then." Tara smiled. "Sandi decided to move on and explore more of the island, but she was a great volunteer. Anyway, I should probably be going. Here's my information."

She wrote her phone number down on a small piece of paper and handed it to me.

"Thanks, Tara. It was an honor to meet you today." I smiled. "Perhaps it was fate, I don't know. Anyway, I'll text you, and we'll go from there."

"Great meeting you, Andrew! Talk to you soon!"

I walked onto the Community grounds, feeling as if a whirlwind had hit me. I'd just found a new opportunity, and it involved the only other skill that approached the strength my computer skills: writing itself.

CHAPTER 28

FLOWER OF LIFE

The more I thought about it, the more excited I felt about working with Tara. In just two weeks, there would be a 10-day silent meditation course, and I got a strong intuitive nudge that I should go. Perhaps it would be the perfect opportunity to renew my mind.

In the midst of these hopeful developments, I met a second person who would go on to change my life. It all started one auspicious lunchtime. I had just bought a few items from Island Naturals market and had sat down at one of the long green tables just outside the store, where a few other people were also eating their lunch. As was my usual pastime when eating lunch there, I ate my food quietly, letting the conversations flow around me.

Talk of farm animals, people new to the island, and occasional emotional therapy sessions were not uncommon. Sometimes I'd hear useful updates, like humpback whales being sighted recently. And sometimes I'd get useless or outdated advice, like the time I followed one guy's instructions on where to find free bananas.

And for some reason, I had listened to him. The only problem was that after I'd pushed through hundreds of meters of forest, all I found was a banana tree that had been picked clean.

One lunchtime at Island Naturals, I saw the vegan gelato makers, Valko and Bijou, walking up to the store, and I waved to them as they passed by. They waved back, saying aloha before they went inside. I'd seen them off and on at Uncle Robert's night market, but I hadn't talked to them as much as I would have liked. I made a mental note to hang out with them more at the market later.

Anansi sat down across from me, and we shared a lunch together as we sometimes did. And when Valko and Bijou reemerged from the store, someone nearby invited them to an event, most likely a party, but they politely declined, heading back out to their car.

I turned to Anansi. "I wonder what they have planned."

"Don't you see?" Anansi said. "Isn't it obvious? They're *beautiful* people. They're not like most of the people here."

His words took me aback, at first. But I had to admit they were pretty fashionable and quite fit, too. Not that I was surprised; most vegans on Hawaii were.

The lunches I spent in front of Island Naturals blur together, but one day in particular was special, when an older woman clad in white called Raziela sat across from me. I had never seen her before, and we got to talking.

To my surprise, Raziela was a fellow author. She told me that she had written many books and was working on a new one, and she grew excited when she heard that I was a web consultant and had made many websites for clients in the past.

She smiled broadly, fine lines forming across her face as she told me about how she could really use my help improving the usability of her website, as well as designing some new covers for her books. It was hard to contain her enthusiasm; she had been on the lookout for someone like me for a while, but apparently someone with my range of skills wasn't easy to find in Puna.

In fact, she was so excited that she asked if I could come and help her after we finished eating, but I already had a previous engagement that afternoon.

We agreed to meet at Uncle Robert's market that night. She gave me her business card, and I immediately noticed that the phone number had been crossed out and a new number was written beside it.

"Yes, my phone number changed. That's my new number! Or you can call me on Skype. I have that on most of the day, too."

I pocketed the card and thanked her again.

"Cool," I said, standing up. "Well, I'll see you at Uncle Robert's tonight then. I think we can come to a good win-win situation." I smiled. "I'm so glad that I randomly met you."

"I don't think it was random," she said. "See you tonight!"

That evening, Uncle Robert's night market was as it always had been: a beautiful, colorful celebration of Hawaiian slack-key guitar music, delicious food, and local crafts.

Toward the front of the market, I grabbed some Thai curry from a family-run booth and found a good place to sit down and enjoy my food, letting the live Hawaiian music wash over me. The sights of the smiling people, the sound of the guitars, and the taste of the fresh food always put me in a good mood.

Afterward, I navigated through the crowd and approached a booth I'd seen a few times before that had always tempted me. For some reason, I'd never stopped there before, but tonight felt like the right time to finally try Valko and Bijou's vegan gelato, which was made from coconut milk instead of cow milk.

Written on a small blackboard over their table was an impressive list of flavors, ranging from rose-petal pistachio to butterscotch sea-salt to chocolate mac-nut.

They all sounded delicious, and I decided to treat myself, talking to the couple behind the counter. They were incredibly sweet and warm, even letting me sample two flavors before I made my final choice. For the life of me, I cannot recall the first vegan gelato flavor I ever tried from them (possibly amaretto almond), but it was the beginning of a beautiful friendship. Their vegan gelato tasted better than any dairy-based ice cream I had ever had, and because it was entirely plant-based, it was healthier for me and the environment, too.

I talked to Valko for a few minutes while his partner Bijou scooped more gelato out of large containers in a cooler, learning that they had been growing the business for almost three years at that point and preferred to use local ingredients. Valko had a real rock-n-roll vibe to him, and I don't think I ever saw him wear anything but black, white, or a shade of grey.

More importantly, he had a warm, welcoming disposition. We got along instantly, and I asked him if they'd be there the following week.

"We're here every week," he said, "and Saturdays we're at SPACE market, too."

I made a mental note to check that market out later, and thanked him.

With a cup of delicious vegan ice cream in my hand, I wandered around the rest of the market, finding an aroma therapy booth, an incense seller who had little baggies of nearly every burnable herb I could think of, and a stunning tie-dye artist, before I recalled that I had planned to meet Raziela at the market, too. But it didn't take me long to find her.

As is the custom on the island, we greeted each other with a hug before discussing the details of how I could help her and at what price. She explained to me that she'd checked out my ratings on Amazon, as well as my website, and was impressed. I decided that charging by the hour was the most fair, and she agreed. She said she wanted to get started as soon as possible, and we made an appointment to meet the following Wednesday.

That night, I left Uncle Robert's with a feeling of bright possibility. I had been so focused on writing my book and my work at the Community that I hadn't even posted any ads to find clients yet, but working with Raziela felt right. And with all the changes happening, some extra cash would come in handy.

In the face of the challenging situation at the Community and the uncertain future of my relationship with Selena, I often welcomed little side-adventures to take my mind off of what was worrying me at the time. While a given side-adventure may not further one of my goals directly, it would often provide me with a useful new perspective or open up hitherto unknown opportunities to me.

In those days, my challenge was to balance my desire for spontaneity with my desire to finish my second book, but with all of the changes happening around me and within me, I only managed to find two days per week to focus on writing. Later, I would learn to be more efficient, but in the midst of so many possibilities, I found it appropriate to divide up my focus into thirds: Community work, island exploration, and writing. And that Friday, I had a productive morning, writing just under a thousand words for the book.

My first book, *The Truth Beyond the Sky*, had just completed a 48-hour free deal the previous night, giving away over a thousand copies of the book in the process. That giveaway would really help spur people to write more reviews of the book, and I finished up my writing session that morning feeling optimistic for the future.

Afterward, I felt that familiar tug in my heart to explore. I also needed some more food, so I did what I usually did: I hiked up to the main road and stuck out my thumb.

As part of this adventure, I met Murrie, who was only a couple years younger than me. As hard as I've tried, I cannot recall exactly where Murrie and I first met. It could have been the beach, the store, or simply along the road.

Murrie was cool, cute, and filled with a youthful enthusiasm that I found refreshing. She had recently finished a long stint work-trading on a sailboat, an adventure that impressed me since most young people probably wouldn't be so bold. She had an adventurous spirit, and after talking a while, we felt like old friends. That day wasn't the first time such a thing had happened to me, but I always welcomed the feeling.

She asked if I wanted to hang out and have lunch with her at the place she was house sitting.

"Sure."

"It's a really cool house," she said. "And the couple said that it's fine to bring a friend over as long as they stay by the living room. They're pretty cool."

She stuck out her thumb, and before long we were in front of a modest house tucked within the rainforest. Inside, I was impressed at the expansiveness of the space. The combined living room and kitchen had hardwood floors and vaulted ceilings, and beyond the kitchen to the right, I saw a screen door that led to an enclosed patio.

Murrie generously pulled out some cheese, grapes, and other things she'd bought from the fridge; and it didn't take long before we had a pretty well-rounded lunch set out on the round dining table. She told me more about the sailing trip she'd just taken, and the conversation flowed effortlessly. I asked her how long she'd been exploring Puna, and it had only been a few months. She hadn't really explored Cinderland or Green Lake yet, and I offered to show her later. She loved the idea.

I asked if we could check out the enclosed patio, and she led me beyond the screen door to where a cozy couch and wooden chairs had been set out. A shallow wooden shelf wrapped around the edge of the patio enclosure, holding a few candles and bottles. Even better, the yellow paneling of the ceiling set the entire patio in a comforting warm hue, and I noticed a hammock hanging from the ceiling at the far end.

Soon, I was sitting on a padded seat at the far end while she swung a bit in the hammock, and we talked some more. It dawned on me that she was flirting with me, that she was interested in more than friendship.

I felt tempted to explore that potential, but my heart still felt mixed up about Selena. Both my heart and my gut said that Selena and I still had a chance.

Murrie was cute and had a good attitude, and I didn't want to hurt her by being emotionally vulnerable one day and then distant and hung up on someone else the following week. I hold myself to a higher standard. If I'm going to explore attraction with someone, I don't want to come across confused, and I had to admit to myself that, for most of that month, I felt quite confused indeed.

In retrospect, I wish I had told her all about it, but I don't think we talked about Selena at all. After all, it wasn't my habit to talk about such things with a girl I'd just met. At the time, I might have felt that it was tacky to give so much information early on. Now, I'm not so sure.

I asked her if she still wanted to go to Cinderland together, and she was excited by the idea. She locked up the house, and we caught a ride out.

Since I was almost always there at night, it often struck me at how different Cinderland looked when I visited it during the daytime. It was even more apparent how thick the jungle was during the day, with thick patches of palm and ti trees obscuring the buildings at every turn, and it took us a couple tries before we found the narrow trail that snaked through the jungle to the most interesting building on the property: the yoga studio.

I had never been inside the yoga studio before, but I knew roughly where it was. After all, it was easily the largest enclosed building on the property. Most of the other structures were frames with tarps, but the yoga studio was completely screened in and pretty tall, allowing for plenty of natural light to filter in from above the forest canopy.

The room was perhaps six by ten meters, and painted in the center was a beautiful mandala pattern, radiating out in four directions along the wooden floor until it became a 12-pointed star enclosed in a huge circle, almost like a compass rose. Hanging from the ceiling above it was a string of Tibetan prayer flags, backlit by the warm afternoon sun.

We looked around in awe of the space, happy that we had the room to ourselves. I noticed a few silks hanging from the ceiling, the kind that one can swing on or do stretches with, and Murrie starting playing with them almost immediately. She put her feet in a few loops at one end and leaned back into a larger loop, tipping her head upside down, smiling at me. I pulled out my camera, and asked her if she wanted a picture.

"Sure!" she said, and I snapped a few.

On the far end of the room, I noticed a small, square painting of the Flower of Life, painted in striking colors and golden lines. It added even more depth to the space, and I wondered who painted it.

After a while, I asked Murrie if she was ready to go check out Green Lake, and we slipped out of Cinderland without much fuss. It was often quiet there in the afternoon, and we hitchhiked the short distance south to the entrance to Green Lake, the only sizable lake on the island that I'd ever heard of.

A sign at the front gate indicated that it was five dollars per person, but I'd heard that if one talked to the woman at the gate, sometimes she would let people in for free.

We slid through the half-open gate and immediately saw the woman, called Hasa, standing behind a fruit stand stacked with small bananas, guava, and coconuts.

Hasa wore her smile as if it were a garment that she donned every morning, well-worn out of love.

She greeted us warmly, and I introduced myself and Murrie, saying that we'd never seen the Green Lake before and had been walking by. We made some small talk for a few minutes, hovering around the threshold of the path ahead, until I found a natural break in the conversation to ask the question that needed to be asked.

"So is it all right if we take a quick look at the lake? We're not going up Green Mountain, just the lake."

Hasa's smile somehow grew even wider, and her sharp eyes scanned us again.

"Sure, sweetie! That's fine. Just be sure to be back before sunset. We close soon."

If I made an audible sigh of relief at that point, I wouldn't be surprised. We both thanked her profusely and made our way down the narrow dirt road ahead which led under a guava tree to a grassy clearing, a wide blue sky above us. On the far end of the clearing, a trail led into the jungle and down.

Once again, we headed under the thick forest canopy, following the narrow trail over thick tree roots that protruded from the dirt of the forest floor. The trail grew steep at points, until we reached a metal gate that was unlocked. The trail leveled out, and ahead we saw a narrow flat area where a few people were sitting.

We walked up to them and quickly realized that they were sitting right at the shore of Green Lake itself. They'd spread out a few towels to sit on and were staring out to someone floating on an orange inflatable raft out in the middle of the lake, a small body of water that was roughly circular. Its surface was half-covered in algae, and green tree branches hung over the entire perimeter of the lake. A small patch of sky could be seen from where we were standing, providing direct sunlight to only a fraction of the surface.

We walked up to the group and introduced ourselves, quickly learning that they were part of a small film company, and they were filming a new movie at Green Lake, a *Creature from the Black Lagoon* kind of film. One woman pointed out the man on the raft, saying that he was the director, and I asked her if I could take a few photos.

She said that was fine, and I took out my camera and maxed out the zoom to get a better view of the director who was, at that moment, lying on his stomach with a camera in hand, paddling clumsily with his flippers to propel himself slowly forward. He splashed as he moved ahead, spraying droplets of water into the air that were caught in the golden afternoon sun, and I took a couple pictures of that, too.

We continued talking and eventually the director made his way back to the shore where two actors were waiting in swimwear, stumbling out of the raft before greeting us warmly. I asked if we might be able to see the film later, and he passed along a website that we could check out.

Small as it was, that was the first actual film crew I'd seen on the island, and I told him I was glad to see some film work being done in Puna. Not many people around had expressed interest in capturing the beauty of Puna in that way, and as they packed up their gear, I wished them all smooth sailing on their film.

As we hiked back up the steep trail and across the wide grassy clearing, I noticed that the sun was getting low in the sky, and at one point I asked Murrie if she would be interested in coming to the meditation course I was taking on September 25. I told her how almost everyone I'd met had said that it was a transformational experience, and since they were holding one right here in Puna, it was pretty convenient, too.

She seemed ambivalent about the idea. Whether it was because she had pledged to house-sit beyond that date or for some other reason, I cannot recall, but I felt disappointed that she wasn't going to share the experience with me. Later, I mentioned the idea to Selena and got a similar response.

Obviously, dedicating 10 days to a meditation course wasn't something that everyone wanted to do, but the closer I grew to that day, the more excited I became.

I thought of Tara and the meeting I had scheduled with her the following Monday. I felt so grateful to have an opportunity to work-trade in a better situation. Even better, it was doing something that I loved, something that I felt *born* to do: **write**.

September 25 was only about two weeks away, and as I hugged Murrie farewell that afternoon and hitchhiked back, my mind turned to the impending meditation retreat.

As I reflected on it, my heart knew that I wouldn't be returning to the Community after that.

For the next two weekends, I just had to keep my head down and be extra conscious of how I dealt with Matangi. Then, Tara and I would iron out the details of our agreement, and I would finally move on, diving into an intense silent meditation course soon after.

Everything was about to change for me.

I couldn't wait.

AFTERWORD

Congratulations for completing VOLUME 1 of *Ten Thousand Hours in Paradise*.

Did you enjoy this book? Let your voice be heard! These days, readers, not publishers, are the gatekeepers.

By leaving a review, **you harness your power** to decide which authors thrive, and I would be forever grateful if you would take a minute to write an honest review on:

- Amazon
- Goodreads
- Or wherever you bought this book!

As an independent author, I depend on the support of readers like you. Rest assured that *Ten Thousand Hours in Paradise* will continue in VOLUME 2 and will conclude in VOLUME 3.

In fact, you can start reading an early draft of VOLUME 2 **right now** when you support me over at my Patreon.com page. For less than the cost of a coffee, you get early access to tons of material, two free ebooks, and the entirety of VOLUME 2, many months before it's released to the public. Plus, you'll get access to dozens of photos mentioned in this book!

As an independent artist, I really appreciate your support! Check out my Patreon page and all bonuses here:

http://bit.ly/hawaiinow

On the next page I've even included a sample of VOLUME 2 for your reading pleasure. And after that, be sure to sign up for my mailinglist so you don't miss any of my upcoming books.

mahalo nui loa,
Andrew M. Crusoe

FREE PREVIEW

TEN THOUSAND HOURS IN PARADISE

VOLUME TWO

THE PROSPECT OF LIVING SOMEWHERE NEW, not to mention a community that valued meditation, brightened my thoughts more and more.

The idea cheered me up so much that I even felt that my communications with Matangi went smoother. After enduring months of scrutiny from her, and seeing her treat other volunteers similarly, it was a relief to realize that soon I wouldn't have to communicate with her at all.

On Monday, Tara and I met in a central place in town before zooming down to the meditation center property, near where the guest house was. That trip was the first time I'd ever been to a center explicitly dedicated to developing a meditation practice, and I wasn't sure what to expect. Whatever it was like, I knew that it would be special. After all, such places cannot help but be special when they're tucked away in the wild jungles of Puna.

More importantly, the Center would be my home for 11 days during the upcoming silent meditation course. And unlike most of the people who would attend, I was about to get a personal tour before the course had even started.

The property wasn't what I had expected. Whether it was the speed with which Tara led me around, the unpredictable landscape, or a bit of both, my first tour of the property was rather disorienting. A thick patch of jungle gave way to a grassy area. Beyond, a central house was the main fixture of the property. Tara led me around a large shrub to where a slender man called Werther was digging in a garden.

"Hello!" he said. "I'd shake your hand but I'm covered in dirt. So you're going to help Tara with her book? That's terrific!"

I smiled back to him. "We're going to have a meeting about it, actually."

Tara had a brief conversation with Werther on how the new gardens were coming along before leading me along the edge of the central field and down another path.

We walked past a small structure and made a sharp left turn toward a patch of tall palm trees that hung over part of the building. The broad green palms shaded a shower stall where a shorter man called Arvo crouched, apparently doing grout work. He had short hair and an air of quietude around him.

I learned that he too was quite valuable to the Center. In fact, Arvo, Werther, and Tara were the main volunteers.

Tara had a shorter conversation with Arvo, and as they talked, I noticed that another shower stall was right behind the first one. Tara explained that this was where the male meditators showered during a meditation course. The female meditators had an area on the other side of the property. Tara thanked Arvo for the great work, and I got the feeling that the tour Tara was giving me served two purposes. On one hand, Tara was getting me excited about the property, but she was also checking up on their progress on the work of the day. Smart.

We made another turn, finding ourselves at the backside of the large central house, where part of the roof extended out to cover a dining area with several wooden tables and benches.

Tara pointed to the only door at eye level. "And in there is the kitchen." She waved me ahead. "Come on. I'll show you the guest house nearby."

I followed her past a sizable garden and across another grassy area. Eventually we reached a tiny house that neighbored the meditation center. Tara led me around the bushes to a pebbled patio and a wooden door which swung open easily, and I soon realized that I was in the kitchen. It was a small kitchen, but it had almost everything. A long countertop provided plenty of space around the large sink, and there was a stove across from me with four burners. But something was missing. What was it?

Find out when the book is available in ebook or paperback: http://myth.li/paradise/

Or start reading the next book **right now**, when you support my work on Patreon. Start reading VOLUME 2 now: http://bit.ly/hawaiinow

HOW TO GET FREE BOOKS

ONE OF MY favorite parts about being an author is that I get to connect with you, my faithful readers.

To do that, I created the **Aravinda Mailinglist**, the most reliable way I've found to keep the lines of communication open. Once or twice per month, I send out a brief update on what's new, including new releases, cover reveals, and book giveaways!

And by signing up, you'll instantly receive your free Sci-Fi Starter Pack. So what are you waiting for?

Sign up here: http://myth.li/newsletter/

see you beachside,
Andrew M. Crusoe